A Caribbean Dozen

For my Mother and Father – C.F.

Acknowledgements

The editors and publishers gratefully acknowledge permission
to use the following material:
By kind permission of John Agard c/o Caroline Sheldon Literary
Agency *Egg and Spoon Race* and *Ballad of Count Laughula* from
Laughter Is an Egg; published by Viking 1990. By kind permission
of Curtis Brown Ltd on behalf of Grace Nichols *For Dilberta*,
For Forest, Ar-a-Rat and *Sun Is Laughing. Isn't My Name Magical?*
© James Berry, 1994; reprinted by permission of the Peters Fraser
& Dunlop Group Ltd. *Bye Now, Letter From Your Special-Big-Puppy-Dog*
and *Letter From Your Kitten-Cat-Almost-Big-Cat* by James Berry from
When I Dance © James Berry 1988. First published by Hamish
Hamilton Children's Books 1988 and in Puffin Books 1990.
Chicken Dinner and *Ode to Twelve Chocolate Bars* © Valerie Bloom,
1992; reprinted by permission of Cambridge University Press from
Duppy Jamboree. Remember © Pamela Mordecai, 1987; reprinted by
permission of Ginn & Company Ltd from *Storypoems – A First
Collection. Morning Break, Charley and Miss Morley's Goat* and
Dancing Poinciana © Telcine Turner, 1977; reprinted by permission
of Macmillan Education Ltd from *Song of the Surreys*.
News © Telcine Turner, 1988; reprinted by permission of
Macmillan Caribbean from *Climbing Clouds*.

While every effort has been made to obtain permission, in some
cases it has been difficult to trace the copyright holders and we
would like to apologize for any apparent negligence.

First published 1994 by Walker Books Ltd
87 Vauxhall Walk, London SE11 5HJ

10 9 8 7 6 5 4 3 2

Text © 1988, 1990 Grace Nichols; 1990 John Agard; 1994
Valerie Bloom, Faustin Charles, Grace Nichols, Telcine Turner,
David Campbell, Opal Palmer Adisa, Marc Matthews,
John Agard, Dionne Brand, Pamela Mordecai, John Lyons,
James Berry, the Frank Collymore Estate

Illustrations © 1994 Cathie Felstead

Photograph credits: Christine Voge (page 79),
Deo Persaud (page 55 and 49)

This book has been typeset in Novarese.

Printed in Hong Kong

British Library Cataloguing in Publication Data
A catalogue record for this book is
available from the British Library

ISBN 0-7445-2172-6

A CARIBBEAN DOZEN

A Collection of Poems

Edited by
John Agard and Grace Nichols

Illustrated by Cathie Felstead

WALKER BOOKS
AND SUBSIDIARIES
LONDON • BOSTON • SYDNEY

Contents

Introduction
by John Agard and Grace Nichols

One of the things we recall about life in the Caribbean is the colourful, bustling markets, with their bargaining and bantering, and the way vendors would throw in an extra fruit or fish or handful of shrimps, especially if you had bought a lot. This bonus or extra bit of freeness is known around the Caribbean by various names such as the "mek-up" or the "brata". In keeping with this tradition, we have thrown an extra poet into your poetry basket – a generous Caribbean dozen of thirteen poets drawn from around the English-speaking Caribbean.

The voices of these poets are informed by the rhythms and flavours and textures of a Caribbean childhood. Though many of them now live in metropolitan places in Britain, Canada and the USA, their formative meeting with the magic of the word happened under tropical skies where fireflies were shooting stars and English nursery rhymes and fairytales mingled with the tricky doings of Anancy spiderman and ghost stories about duppies and jumbies with turned-back feet.

We've had great pleasure in putting these poets together and hope A *Caribbean Dozen* brings you dozens of delight.

Our house, in a small village in the middle of Jamaica, was full of children. I was the second of nine brothers and sisters, so there was always someone to play with. Various cousins came to live with us at one time or another, and this meant it was possible to play the ring games that needed six or more people. Best of all, though, I liked the skipping games, and I sometimes use the rhymes from these in my poems now. I was first introduced to poetry by my grandmother, mother and elder brother, while I was still at infant school. My brother would recite to me the poems he'd learnt at school and I loved it.

Valerie Bloom

My primary school was about four miles from home, but the roads were poor and sometimes there was no transport, so we would have a long walk. My favourite subject was English because I was good at it. I read a lot, and as soon as I started school I joined the local library. I can still remember the first book I borrowed – it was called Are You My Mother? and was about a baby chick looking for its mother. I enjoyed school but I enjoyed the holidays more, especially the eight weeks in summer when we could put hampers on our donkey and go into the hills to pick ripe mangoes. We would set off home, our hampers laden with fruit. For a couple of days we'd eat our fill, then we'd be off into the hills again. Bliss!

WATER EVERYWHERE

There's water on the ceiling,
And water on the wall,
There's water in the bedroom,
And water in the hall,
There's water on the landing,
And water on the stair,
Whenever Daddy takes a bath
There's water everywhere.

CHICKEN DINNER

Mama, don' do it, please,
Don' cook dat chicken fe dinner,
We know dat chicken from she hatch,
She is de only one in de batch
Dat de mongoose didn' catch,
Please don' cook her fe dinner.

Mama, don' do it, please,
Don' cook dat chicken fe dinner,
Yuh mean to tell mi yuh feget
Yuh promise her to we as a pet
She not even have a chance to lay yet
An yuh want to cook her fe dinner.

Mama, don' do it, please,
Don' cook dat chicken fe dinner,
Don' give Henrietta de chop,
Ah tell yuh what, we could swop,
We will get yuh one from de shop,
If yuh promise not to cook her fe dinner.

Mama, me really glad, yuh know,
Yuh never cook Henny fe dinner,
An she glad too, ah bet,
Oh Lawd, me suddenly feel upset,
Yuh don' suppose is somebody else pet
We eating now fe dinner?

LUCKY ME

Grass and carrots for the rabbit,
Seeds and grain for the turkey,
Some parboiled figs
Will do for the pigs,
But all the best foods for me.

One tiny hutch for the rabbit,
One little coop for the turkey,
I can't think why
Pigs love a sty,
But it's a nice big house for me.

They make a stew out of the rabbit,
And Christmas dinner from the turkey,
Pigs are taken
For ham and bacon,
But nobody dares eat me.

ODE TO TWELVE CHOCOLATE BARS

Oh glorious doz
That woz.

WHO DAT GIRL?

Who dat wide-eye likkle girl
Staring out at me?
Wid her hair in beads an' braids
An' skin like ebony?

Who dat girl, her eye dem bright
Like night-time peeny-wallie?
Wid Granny chain dem circle roun'
Her ankle, neck, an' knee?

Who dat girl in Mummy's shoes,
Waist tie wid Dad's hankie?
Who dat girl wid teeth like pearl
Who grinning out at me?

Who dat girl? Who dat girl?
Pretty as poetry?
Who dat girl in de lookin'-glass?

Yuh mean dat girl is me?

As a child I loved listening to folk tales told by the old people in our seaside village on the north coast of Trinidad. My grandmother was my favourite storyteller. She introduced me to the Bible and told me local, and other, nursery rhymes. She had a magical way of making stories and poems come alive. I cannot remember being taught to read and write; I guess they came as naturally to me as breathing. At primary and secondary schools I was always top of my class in essay writing and literature. I was good at reciting poetry too, and my teachers wanted me to enter the island-wide Recitation Contest – but at thirteen I was too shy. The subjects I had most difficulty with were maths and

Faustin Charles

science, and because I hated them I never worked very hard at them. The first books I fell in love with were Grimms' Fairy Tales, Andersen's Fairy Tales and The Town Mouse and the Country Mouse, which I received as a school prize. I began making up my own stories and poems from about the age of seven, telling them to my friends. I had my first essay accepted by a national Trinidad newspaper when I was twenty-two and my first book of poems was published four years later. I have since completed several more.

GREEN JEWELS

Suppose all the children
In the world turned green,
Green eyes, green hair, green colour!
Speaking in green voices everywhere;
The trees would be their mothers,
Summer would be their fathers,
And every night before they go to sleep
A black-eyed fairy will reap
Raindrops from their dreams
To keep them fresh and clean.

The Runner

Run, run, runner man,
As fast as you can,
Faster than the speed of light,
Smoother than a bird in flight.
Run, run, runner man,
No one can catch the runner man,
Swifter than an arrow,
Outrunning his own shadow.
Run, run, runner man,
Faster than tomorrow.
Run, run, runner man,
Quicker than a rocket!
Into deep space spinning a comet!
Run, run, runner man,
Lighting the heavens of the night,
Run, run, runner man,
Out of sight,
Run, run, runner man, run!

Steel Band Jump Up

I put my ear to the ground,
And I hear the steel-band sound:
Ping pong! Ping pong!
Music deep, rhythm sweet,
I'm dancing tracking the beat;
Like a seashell's ringing song,
Ping pong! Ping pong!
Moving along, moving along,
High and low, up and down,
Ping pong! Ping pong!
Pan beating singing, round and round,
Ping pong! Ping pong!

THE CAT WHO COULD FLY

Every night he flies from the window-sill,
Over the hill,
Purring dizzily at the full moon,
Circling the land, valleys, rivers and the sea;
Only thunder brings him down to earth
To an old lady's chamber.
In the daytime he sings sad songs,
And the world is silent,
For he cuts all tongues,
Sharper than a knife,
From miaowing the nine secrets of his life.

The cat who could fly,
Never told a lie
And drank all tears
From the old lady's eyes.

BRAZILIAN FOOTBALLER

Pelé kicked in his mother's belly!
And the world shouted:
Goooooooooooooooooooooooooooooooooal!
When her son was born,
He became the sun,
And rolled on the fields of heaven.
The moon and stars trained and coached him,
In the milky way
He swayed, danced and dribbled,
Smooth like water off a duck's back
Ready always to attack.
One hot day, heaven fell down, floored!
Through the Almighty's hands
Pelé had scored!

I spent my small-girl days in a country village on the east coast of Guyana and my most treasured memory is of myself, around the age of six, standing calf-deep in goldish-brown water, watching fish go by just below the sunlit surface. When I was eight years old I moved with my five sisters, one brother, mother, father and grandmother to the city, Georgetown, with its white wooden buildings, bustling markets and famous St George's Cathedral (said to be the highest wooden building in the world). My father was a headmaster and my mother enjoyed playing the piano at home and loved having people around her. I can't remember a single day when our home wasn't visited

Grace Nichols

by friends or neighbours or relatives who had dropped in "just fuh a minute" but ended up staying hours, telling jokes and stories and sharing in whatever was cooked. I joined the Public Free Library when we moved to Georgetown and read my fill of Enid Blyton, William, Nancy Drew, and the Hardy Boys mysteries, much to the despair of our librarians who recommended other kinds of literature. But I did get a taste of "other literature", including poetry, from books at home. I can actually remember one of the first words I fell in love with — "excruciating"! I must have been about nine or ten, reading a William book in bed. William had just delivered a pinch under the table to some not-very-nice person's leg. The person shot up in "excruciating" pain. Apart from laughing, I remember savouring the sound of the word. I still get great pleasure from the sound of words.

FOR DILBERTA

(*Biggest of the elephants at London Zoo*)

The walking-whale
of the earth kingdom – Dilberta.

The one whose waist
your arms won't get around – Dilberta.

The mammoth one whose weight
you pray won't knock you to the ground.

The one who displays toes
like archway windows,
bringing the pads of her feet down
like giant paperweights
to keep the earth from shifting about.

Dilberta, rippling as she ambles under
the wrinkled tarpaulin of her skin,
casually throwing the arm of her nose,
saying, "Go on, have a stroke."

But sometimes, in her mind's eye,
Dilberta gets this idea – she could be a moth!
Yes, with the wind stirring behind her ears,
she could really fly.

Rising above the boundaries of the paddock,
Making for the dark light of the forest –
Hearing, O once more, the trumpets roar.

FOR FOREST

Forest could keep secrets
Forest could keep secrets

Forest tune in every day
to watersound and birdsound
Forest letting her hair down
to the teeming creeping of her forest-ground

But Forest don't broadcast her business
no Forest cover her business down
from sky and fast-eye sun
and when night come
and darkness wrap her like a gown
Forest is a bad dream woman

Forest dreaming about mountain
and when earth was young
Forest dreaming of the caress of gold
Forest roosting with mysterious eldorado

and when howler monkey
wake her up with howl
Forest just stretch and stir
to a new day of sound

but coming back to secrets
Forest could keep secrets
Forest could keep secrets
          And we must keep Forest

AR-A-RAT

I know a rat on Ararat,
He isn't thin, he isn't fat
Never been chased by any cat
Not that rat on Ararat.
He's sitting high on a mountain breeze,
Never tasted any cheese,
Never chewed up any old hat,
Not that rat on Ararat.
He just sits alone on a mountain breeze,
Wonders why the trees are green,
Ponders why the ground is flat,
O that rat on Ararat.
His eyes like saucers, glow in the dark –
The last to slip from Noah's ark.

SUN IS LAUGHING

This morning she got up
on the happy side of bed,
pulled back
the grey sky-curtains
and poked her head
through the blue window
of heaven,
her yellow laughter
spilling over,
falling broad across the grass,
brightening the washing on the line,
giving more shine
to the back of a ladybug
and buttering up all the world.

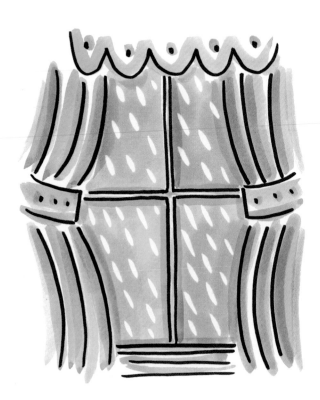

Then, without any warning,
as if she was suddenly bored,
or just got sulky
because she could hear no one
giving praise
to her shining ways,
Sun slammed the sky-window close,
plunging the whole world
into greyness once more.

O Sun, moody one,
how can we live
without the holiday of your face?

I grew up in the Bahamas. Milton Street, off Market Street, New Providence Island, was my birthplace. As a child I was sickly, and hence reserved. Comics, books and newspapers were my frequent companions, although I developed many lasting friendships. Pets I recall include Cluck-Cluck the hen, Princess the goat, Mixie the cat, and dogs Sundae, Maestro and Star. "Babylon", the yard where I spent much of my childhood and adolescence, would now be called a ghetto or slum, but at that time we weren't too conscious of such terms. Generally, my extended family and neighbours were friendly and witty. A golden wall loomed up along the northern side of

Telcine Turner

Babylon. It enclosed a wonderful place — a combination of movie theatre, nightclub and living quarters for the owner, a retired dancer who walked in the middle of the road like a god. It wasn't until his tragic death that we learned of his world-wide fame. As children we admired the fascinating murals, tiles and gardens in that forbidden golden mansion. It was the singing I heard from there along with songs played on the radio in the Fifties that ignited my interest in words and music.

NEWS

"Mummy, hey Mummy,
  bet you can't guess what happened
  right after I bathed off
  and shampooed my hair…"

"Good for you, dumpling.
  You're finished; that's something.
  Now you will need
  some pyjamas to wear."

"Mummy, oh Mummy,
  I can't wait to tell you –
  I combed out my hair
  then I brushed *all* my teeth…"

"I'm proud of you, precious,
  you do look delicious.
  Go to the drawer
  and get socks for your feet."

"Mummy, please Mummy,
  look here in my mouth.
  When I flossed like you told me
  my jaw tooth flew out!"

32

MORNING BREAK

Girls in white blouses, blue skirts,
boys in blue trousers, white shirts,
singing, swinging, screeching, reaching,
hooking wasps, riddle-saying,
ring-playing –

Bayhanna, bayhanna, bayhanna, bay.
If your teachers scold you
Listen to what they say.
That's the way you bayhanna, bayhanna, bay.

Lamppost schoolmaster in grey jacket,
grey tales of wild Abaco hog and donkey;
mild worry, calm hurry,
stiff bones and cane;
ring-playing –

Round the green apple tree
Where the grass grows so sweet,
Miss Della, Miss Della,
Your true lover was here,
And he wrote you a letter
To turn 'round your head.

First bell, all frozen.
Second bell, instant motion.
Disappear.

33

CHARLEY AND MISS MORLEY'S GOAT

Charley's mother went to town
Run, Charley, run
With a red hat on and a purple gown.
Run, Charley, run

Before she left she told the boys,
Run, Charley, run
"You all stay home and play with your toys."
Run, Charley, run

Charley's brother and sister too
Run, Charley, run
Cleaned up the yard. What did he do?
Run, Charley, run

He dashed with friends up and down the street.
Run, Charley, run
Then Miss Morley's goat they began to beat.
Run, Charley, run

The goat cried, "Ma-a-a!" Miss Morley woke.
Run, Charley, run
When she saw the boys she was vexed and spoke:
Run, Charley, run

34

"Why don't you leave my goat alone?"
Run, Charley, run
"Charles, I'll tell your mother when she comes home."
Run, Charley, run

Bad as her word, when the jitney brought Mom,
Run, Charley, run
Miss Morley told her about her son.
Run, Charley, run

Under the bed, Charley heard Mom say,
Run, Charley, run
"I'm going to fix his skin today!"
Run, Charley, run

"Come out here, Charles, and I mean RIGHT NOW."
Run, Charley, run
"Who told you to leave this yard, anyhow?"
Run, Charley, run

Charley was spanked and sent to bed
Run, Charley, run
For not doing what his mama said.
Run, Charley, run

DANCING POINCIANA

Fire in the treetops,
Fire in the sky.
Blossoms red as sunset
Dazzling to the eye.

Dance, Poinciana,
Sway, Poinciana,
On a sea of green.
Dance, Poinciana,
Sway, Poinciana,
Regal as a queen.

Fire in the treetops,
Fire in the sky.
Crimson petals and white
Stained with scarlet dye.

Dance, Poinciana,
Sway, Poinciana,
On a sea of green.
Dance, Poinciana,
Sway, Poinciana,
Regal as a queen.

I grew up on the banks of a wide river in Guyana in South America. Like all the other children on the river I learnt to swim and paddle a canoe at a very early age. We must have been very brave or else we didn't understand the dangers around us, for in that river and in the water places nearby were stingrays, alligators, electric eels and the largest snakes in the world — water boa constrictors, or "camudis" as we called them. One of them swallowed my grandfather's dog, Bunty, which was about the size of an Alsatian. In and around our house, on the river banks, there were wasps, scorpions, tarantulas and even snakes, and in the nearby forests, monkeys, baboons, tiger cats and jaguars. I survived all that and became a singer/songwriter and poet when I grew up.

David Campbell

With my guitar I travelled to many places including Sweden, England, Wales, Scotland, Ireland, Holland, Germany, the United States, Central America and right across the big country where I now live, Canada. I have made my home where the mountains meet the Pacific Ocean, in Vancouver. In this city you can see eagles soaring in the sky and mountain tops that are still wild. You can walk for miles by the ocean and through wide green places. I love living here.

CORN AND POTATO

The corn and potato, peanut, strawberry:
Who gave them to us, can anyone tell me?
Canoes and snowshoes, hammocks for swinging:
Where did they come from in the beginning?

Was it Wonder Woman? No, No,
Six Million Dollar Man? No, No, No,
Was it Tom and Jerry? No, No,
Sylvester and Tweety? No, No, No,
Then was it Max B. Nimble? No, No,
Rocky and Bullwinkle? No, No, No,
Then was it Spiderman? No, No,
It must be Superman! No, No, No, No, No!

Next time you eat your strawberry jam
And peanuts, just ask your daddy this question:
Where did these come from? I'll give you one clue:
It wasn't Archie Bunker, that's all I can tell you.

38

Was it Paul Bunyan? No, No,
Was it Abraham Lincoln? No, No, No,
Francisco Pizarro? No, No,
Was it Robinson Crusoe? No, No, No,
Was it a Pilgrim Father? No, No,
Or an old fur trader? No, No, No,
Columbus or Champlain? No, No,
Tennille and the Captain? No, No, No,
I give up, won't you tell me? Yes, Yes, Yes, Yes, Yes!

If you can't guess then I'd better tell you
Listen to me, I don't want to fool you
Before Columbus, before the Pilgrims,
These things and more all came from the Indians.

The Mic-Mac, the Sarcee, Yes, Yes,
Ojibway and Plains Cree, Yes, Yes, Yes,
The Sioux and the Cheyenne, Yes, Yes,
Apache and Peigan, Yes, Yes, Yes,
The Arawak or Taino, Yes, Yes,
The Mapuche, the Saulteaux, Yes, Yes, Yes,
The Hopi, the Haida, Yes, Yes,
The Inca, the Maya, Yes, Yes, Yes, Yes, Yes!
(I said Yes! Yes! Yes!)

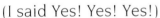

39

ALL THE ONES THEY CALL LOWLY

Garter snake, garter snake, you hurt no one;
You move on so gracefully through the grass.
Garter snake, garter snake, I'll be your friend
And not run away as you pass.

Grasshopper, grasshopper, hopping so high
Away from our crazy feet close to you;
Grasshopper, grasshopper, I'll be your friend;
I wish I could hop as high as you.

Speckled frog, speckled frog, I like your pad;
I don't believe I'll catch warts from you.
Speckled frog, speckled frog, I'll be your friend;
Why should I be frightened of you?

Wriggly worm, wriggly worm, get back inside –
A robin is waiting to take you home;
Wriggly worm, wriggly worm, I'll be your friend;
Above ground you'll not be alone.

All the ones that they do call lowly,
That do no harm to you or me –
Each will be my secret buddy
On grass and water, sand and tree.

THE POW-WOW DRUM

Long black braids and silken shawls
Moving side by side where the eagle calls,
Answering the beat of the pow-wow drum
we come again
to dance again

Hey-a, Hey-a, Hey-a, Hey-a, Hey!
Hey-a, Hey-a, Hey-a, Hey-a, Hey!

Leave the dusty cities far behind,
Meet our brothers of the country with one mind,
Travelling from the east, north, south and west
we come again
to dance again

Chorus

Watching close the feet of lightning fly
Fancy dancers free underneath the sky,
Joining in the circle moving round and round
we come again
to dance again

Chorus

Women shining like the morning sun,
Children making rainbows as they laugh and run,
The old and young meeting like they did long ago
we come again
to dance again

Chorus

The sea has always been, and remains, important to me. As a child, my family went to the beach almost every Sunday. When I was thirteen my poem, "The Sounds I Like to Hear", was published and, not surprisingly, that poem talked about the sea. I grew up primarily on sugar estates, because my father was a chemist and worked in the sugar refineries converting cane juice into rum, and my mother was an executive secretary managing the estate offices. My older sister and I were very close and we got up to lots of mischief. There was always lots of open space where we lived and

Opal Palmer Adisa

there was nothing I loved more than running through the fields and among the tall grasses, then lying on my back and imagining different animals in the clouds. I spent many summers in a small village with my mother's relatives, and that experience is one that I'll never forget. My Aunt Zilla was a great teller of Duppy (ghost) and Anancy stories. Often, when she'd finished, especially if it was a dark, moonless night, I would be so scared I wouldn't move without someone walking with me. I seem to remember always writing, or at least making up stories and poems in my head. I still make up stories that I tell to my two daughters, Shola and Teju, and my son, Jawara. Now Shola, who is seven, is herself a great storyteller. I enjoy all sorts of writing, from academic essays, to poetry, to children's stories.

BEING A TREE

One time
I stood on the arm of the sofa
balancing on one leg
my arms spread wide
like branches.

I was a gigantic tree
in the deep green forest.
Many birds sat on my branches
chirping their happy songs.
Small animals nestled by my trunk
prancing and playing, being free.
And just as a blue jay
was about to land on my branch
Mom shouted, "Be careful!"
The blue jay flew away.
I fell, and my tree toppled over.

De More de Merrier

sitting on the
window-sill
looking down
on the street
watching folks
go by
wanting
to be there
in the midst
of it all
but stuck up
here all by myself
no friend
no sister
no brother
not even a dog
to talk to

mama off
somewhere
doing chores
papa still
at work

just me
all by myself
warned not to
go anywhere
told not
to let anyone in
not even a friend
especially if
he's a boy

rules
nothing but rules
not allowed
to choose
not allowed
to decide for myself

i guess
the more the merrier
only applies
to relatives
who come to visit
on holidays

FRUITS

mangoes
and ripe bananas
jelly coconut
and pomegranates
jack-fruit
and stinking-toe
june plum
and nase-berry
sweetsop
and sour-sop
tamarind
and jimbeli
cane-juice
and coolie-plum
star-apple
and custard-apple
navel orange
and wild cherries

fruits everywhere
brimming with life
spread out in front
of market women
buy some
and experience delight

I Am the One

I am the one
who comes out
after dark.
My loveliness
rarer than
a black rose.
With me beauty
is not merely skin deep.
My eyes
pool of deep ocean waters
glittering under the sun.

To others
I am a ray
on a cold bleak day
Forever a daffodil
Penetrating as a needle
Brilliant as diamond.

I dine
with the moon and stars
allowing them to gaze
at my grace.

I am fragrant jasmine
innovative as the traffic light
Ancient as Timbuktu.

Yes, I am the one
Cool and protective
I'm a child of the night .

My homeland is the South American country which the Arawak Indians named Guyana, "Place of Many Waters". We're part of the Caribbean, but we share gigantic rivers and rainforests with our continental neighbours, Brazil, Venezuela and Surinam. As a child I lived on the Berbice River at Bartica and later on the Demerara, which means "gold" and gives its name to the golden brown sugar and rum. I was born during the Second World War, a time of "Grow More Food" posters and battle news on the radio. While growing up I had all sorts of nicknames like Marco, Tallboy, Speedy, but to my family I was simply MC. My storehouse of

Marc Matthews

happy childhood memories includes family performances, plays, poetry recitals and singsongs, and my pets – a turtle called Criptocks and dogs called Paddy, Spliff and Cinco. One thing I will never forget is my return home from England after ten years and four letters away. I was riding through my old neighbourhood when the grandmother of my age-mate Hank leaned out of the window and shouted, "Mac'o, is you boy? Come here!" Then she sent a child to gather my old friends, and started the welcome party. The feeling I had then is the feeling I get now every time I hear the theme song from Cheers, "Where Everybody Knows Your Name".

BOATS

long boats and short boats
fat boats and narrow boats
boats with motors
boats with sails
boats with paddles
boats with steam

boats in rivers
boats in seas
boats in canals
boats in streams
boats made of wood
boats made of steel
boats made of skins
but none can beat
my boat made from
half a dry coconut
skin

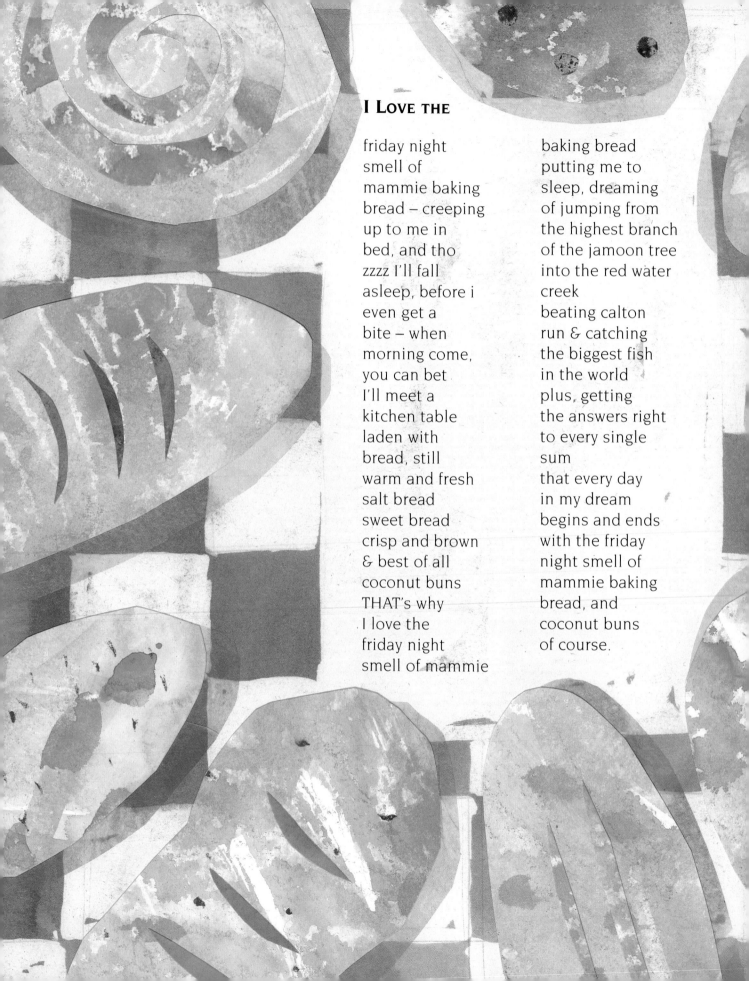

I Love the

friday night
smell of
mammie baking
bread – creeping
up to me in
bed, and tho
zzzz I'll fall
asleep, before i
even get a
bite – when
morning come,
you can bet
I'll meet a
kitchen table
laden with
bread, still
warm and fresh
salt bread
sweet bread
crisp and brown
& best of all
coconut buns
THAT's why
I love the
friday night
smell of mammie
baking bread
putting me to
sleep, dreaming
of jumping from
the highest branch
of the jamoon tree
into the red water
creek
beating calton
run & catching
the biggest fish
in the world
plus, getting
the answers right
to every single
sum
that every day
in my dream
begins and ends
with the friday
night smell of
mammie baking
bread, and
coconut buns
of course.

ME AND MY BALL

Ball jump off of my window-sill
Ball jump off of the floor
Ball jump over granny chair
Ball jump off of the door
Ball jump into granny lap
Ball make granny stop snore

53

A SHOWER A SHAVE A SHAMPOO A CHIN

Sometimes in the bathroom
where I can't be seen
with Daddy's shaving brush
lather my face with his cream

take the razor from out of
his shaver, to shave myself
when I'm finished, with his
aftershave lotion wash my
face clean.

Then put on his favourite slippers
sit in his favourite chair, pick up
a big newspaper and make Mummy
burs' a laugh when I call out
"How about a cup of coffee out here,
my dear."

54

As a little boy I liked listening to cricket on the radio. I'd try to imitate the famous voice of the commentator, John Arlott. I'd make up pretend commentaries about a batsman hooking "majestically" and "magnificently", not realizing that I myself was becoming hooked on the sound of words. My primary school was called St Mary's and it faced a big Roman Catholic cathedral called Brickdam. The boys wore short khaki trousers with navy blue shirts, and the girls wore navy blue skirts with white sailor-collar tops. Since there was no winter, our teachers often took us outdoors, especially for subjects like drawing and nature study. I liked it when we went into the avenues lined with flamboyant, red-flowered trees,

John Agard

and our teacher would have us chanting multiplication tables and things like "Thirty days hath September, April, June and November…" This was back in my home city of Georgetown, Guyana. My secondary school, St Stanislaus, was also Roman Catholic and most of our teachers were priests. Our O-level English teacher was Father Maxwell. We called him Maxy. He made a big impression on us because he seemed to know every word in the dictionary and once assembled a transistor radio in a soap dish. Maxy made the dictionary such fun that English became my favourite subject, especially writing essays. I also liked taking part in plays. At fourteen I was Captain Hook in Peter Pan. But it wasn't until I got into the sixth form that I remember writing my first poem.

BALLAD OF COUNT LAUGHULA

Dead on the stroke of the midday bell
Count Laughula rises
from his merry shell.

Midday sky resounds with a crack
and Count Laughula plans
another side-splitting attack.

Draped in pudding-yellow cloak
that wobbles in the wind
Count Laughula sharpens a deadly joke.

This is a Count that does not haunt by night
but prefers to stalk a victim
in broad daylight.

When a judge throws off his wig and laughs HA-HA-HA
you can bet he's been bitten
by none other than Count Laughula.

When your teacher gets stitches in her side
and leans on the desk
you know she has been Count Laughula's bride.

When a Prime Minister demands a lollipop
in the middle of a speech
Count Laughula is surely getting on top.

He is the vampire that makes you laugh
and all over the city
he'd sign his mysterious autograph.

And when sun goes down, hook or crook,
Count Laughula returns to his shell
safely tucked in with a comic book.

WHAT THE TEACHER SAID WHEN ASKED:
WHAT ER WE AVIN FOR GEOGRAPHY, MISS?

This morning I've got too much energy
much too much for geography

I'm in a high mood
so class don't think me crude
but you can stuff latitude and longitude

I've had enough of the earth's crust
today I want to touch the clouds

Today I want to sing out loud
and tear all maps to shreds

I'm not settling for river beds
I want the sky and nothing less

Today I couldn't care if east turns west
Today I've got so much energy
I could do press-ups on the desk
but that won't take much out of me

Today I'll dance on the globe
in a rainbow robe

while you class remain seated
on your natural zone
with your pens and things
watching my contours grow wings

All right, class, see you later.
If the headmaster asks for me
say I'm a million dreaming degrees
beyond the equator

a million dreaming degrees
beyond the equator

DISTANCES

The astronaut stared for long into outer space
But could not stare too long at his own face.

EGG-AND-SPOON RACE

One school sports day,
in the egg-and-spoon race,
    the egg ran away
    from the spoon.

The egg brought first place
but judges said: "Let's disqualify
the egg.
It should have waited on the spoon."

The egg said: "Why not disqualify
the spoon
for not catching up with me?
I'll never understand the mystery
    of the human race."

WHEN ANANCY SAY

When Anancy say walk
yuh better run

When Anancy say talk
yuh better dumb

When Anancy say come
yuh better go

When Anancy say quick
yuh better slow

When Anancy say wet
yuh better dry

When Anancy say true
yuh better lie

60

I was born deep in the south of Trinidad in a village called Guayguayare. Our house was so close to the ocean that when the tide came in the pillow tree logs on which the house stood were almost covered by surf. When I was four or so my grandmother, who brought me up, moved to San Fernando, but every holiday we would return to Guaya where my grandfather lived. It is the place I remember and love most. I now live in Toronto, Canada, but each time I go back to Trinidad I always go to Guayguayare just to see the ocean there, to breathe in the smell of copra drying and wood burning and fish frying. In the Sixties, when I was in elementary and high

Dionne Brand

schools, none of the books we studied were about Black people's lives; they were about Europeans, mostly the British. But I felt that Black people's experiences were as important and as valuable, and needed to be written down and read about. This is why I became a writer. In San Fernando I went to a girls' high school where I was taught that girls could use their intellect to live a full life. My teachers and friends there helped me to see that women should enjoy the same rights and freedoms as men. When I moved to Canada in 1970 I joined the civil rights, feminist and socialist movements. I was only seventeen but I already knew that to live freely in the world as a black woman I would have to involve myself in political action as well as writing.

SKIPPING ROPE SONG

Salt, vinegar, mustard, pepper,
If I dare,
I can do better,
who says no?
'cause hens don't crow!
Salt, vinegar, mustard, pepper.

Salt, vinegar, mustard, pepper.
I wanna be great,
a hotshot lawyer,
a famous dancer,
a tough operator,
Salt, vinegar, mustard, pepper.

Salt, vinegar, mustard, pepper,
If I dare
I can do better,
who cares from zero,
that hens don't crow,
Salt, vinegar, mustard, pepper.

RIVER

Take the clothes to the river
beat them on the stones
Sing some songs to the river
praise its deep green face
But don't go where river meets sea
there's a fight going on.
The fight is blue and green and gold,
the current is strong and foamy
'Cause river wants to go to sea
but sea won't be her boat.

WIND

I pulled a hummingbird out of the sky one day
but let it go,
I heard a song and carried it with me
on my cotton streamers,
I dropped it on an ocean and lifted up a wave
with my bare hands,
I made a whole canefield tremble and bend
as I ran by,
I pushed a soft cloud from here to there,
I hurried a stream along a pebbled path,
I scooped up a yard of dirt and hurled it
in the air,
I lifted a straw hat and sent it flying,
I broke a limb from a guava tree,
I became a breeze, bored and tired,
and hovered and hung and rustled and lay
where I could.

HURRICANE

Shut the windows
Bolt the doors
Big rain coming
Climbing up the mountain

Neighbours whisper
Dark clouds gather
Big rain coming
Climbing up the mountain

Gather in the clotheslines
Pull down the blinds
Big wind rising
Coming up the mountain

Branches falling
Raindrops flying
Treetops swaying
People running
Big wind blowing
Hurricane! on the mountain.

OLD MEN OF MAGIC

Old men of magic
with beards long and aged,
speak tales on evenings,
tales so entrancing,
we sit and listen,
to whispery secrets
about the earth and the heavens.
And late at night,
after sundown they speak
of spirits that live
in silk cotton trees,
of frightening shadows
that sneak through the dark,
and bright balls of fire
that fly in night air,
of shapes unimaginable,
we gasp and we gape,
then just as we're scared
old men of magic
wave hands rough and wrinkled
and all trace of fear disappears.

The raw salt smell of the sea and Christmas cakes baked in the big brick "outside" ovens, and ham and puddings boiled in kerosene tins in the backyard... These are some of my early memories of Kingston, Jamaica, where I grew up. I was born in my grandparents' house, next door to the police headquarters and not far from the sea. I remember seeing at least one sea cow (manatee) beached there. Also, I remember it was a wonderful, very old house with a parlour, blinds, wooden floors and a huge open cellar, with a holly bush at the bottom of the stairs in front. It wasn't the house where we lived, but for me it will always be the house of

Pamela Mordecai

my childhood. Nearly every night before we went to bed, my father would read to us from The Best Loved Poems of the American People. He still has the book, and now he's very ill I read him the same poems he used to read to us. The poems had wonderful rhymes and rhythms and some were very sad. I always say that if I write poetry "is my Daddy start it". At school I took part in the All-Island Poetry Competition organized by the Jamaica Poetry League, and learnt many Caribbean poems to recite – especially those of Louise Bennett-Coverley, Jamaica's great poet/actress, known as Miss Lou. I also say that if I write poetry "is because of Miss Lou". Inside I'm still about three and a half – which is maybe why I like writing poems and stories for children. I believe that God lives and speaks through poems and stories.

REMEMBER

Remember when
the world was tall
and you were small
and legs were all
you saw?

Jumping legs
prancing legs
skipping legs
dancing legs.

Thin legs
fat legs
dog legs
cat legs.

Shoes-and-sock legs
on the rocks legs.

Table legs
chair legs
dark legs
fair legs.

Standing-very-tall legs
running-all-around legs.

Stooping-very-small legs
lying-on-the-ground legs.

Quick legs
slow legs
nowhere-
to-go legs.

Remember when
the world was tall
and you were small
and legs were all
you saw?

RABBIT POEM

To keep
a rabbit
is a good
habit.

A rabbit is truly curious:
his eyes are soft
but his whiskers wiggle
and his nose twitches
and his ears jiggle

and his tail
is a bump
on
his rump.

A rabbit
is cheerful
but not especially
careful
about multiplying:
the answers
he gets
to the simple
sum
of one and one
are mystifying…

A rabbit is easy
to care for:
to munch on grass
is what he's hare for.

So if you get
the chance
to have a rabbit,
grab it!

LAMENT OF AN ARAWAK CHILD

Once I played with the hummingbirds
and sang songs to the sea
I told my secrets to the waves
and they told theirs to me.

Now there are no more hummingbirds
the sea's songs are all sad
for strange men came and took this land
and plundered all we had.

They made my people into slaves
they worked us to the bone
they battered us and tortured us
and laughed to hear us groan.

Today we'll take a long canoe
and set sail on the sea
we'll steer our journey by the stars
and find a new country.

QUAO

Quao
is a
lizard.
He is a
wizard
at catching
flies
and other
insects
of minimal
size
who happen
to fall
in his way.
If you are
small,
then,
it would

NOT
be wise
to go
near
Quao.

The first four years of my life were spent in the commercial quarter of Port-of-Spain, Trinidad, with all its bustle, noise and sharp smells. It was here that I saw my first carnival, which I found both frightening and exciting. The music seemed to enter my body; and Jab Molassi with his devil mask was horrifying. When I was about six we moved to the outskirts of the city where it was green and open, and where I really began to enjoy school. School for me then was play, poetry recitation, singing, drawing and nature study. All the other subjects were a bore. I loved the Caribbean folk tales and the poems in my Nelson Reader, *many of which I had to learn by heart. On moonlit nights we scared each other with supernatural tales of La Diablesse, Soucouyant and the Jumbies. Encouraged by my Aunt Christine I discovered the wonderful world of books. Sir Walter Scott was one of my favourite authors. After reading* Quentin Durward *my grandma's healthy banana plant, laden with unripe fruit, suffered a fatal thrust of my wooden sword in a one-sided duel. It was, I believe, this desire to relive the adventures in the books I read that led me to write my first short story and eventually to become a writer and poet. But all those brightly-coloured illustrations from books in my early childhood gave me a love of art and design as well, which led me to become a painter.*

John Lyons

THE PUM NA-NA FROGS

"Pum na-na,"
say the frogs
on a rainy season night
when the moon is bright.

"Pum, pum, pum-na-na,
pum, pum, pum-na-na."
They sit in their muddy pools
thinking
that candleflies
are shooting stars.

CHICKICHONG

My cheeky chickichong
giddying-up with tipsy butterflies
zigzagging over zinnias.

In the shut-in gallery
I am as free as my brown paper kite
playing with the wind,
tail a crazy thing
without zwill,
without sting,
zingaytaying
in a whistled
breeze.

MAMMIE'S COO-COO AND CALLALOO

Every Sunday
Mammie cook coo-coo and callaloo.

Sometimes, there's
peas and rice and salt-beef stew;

I don't know what I would do
without Mammie's coo-coo and callaloo.

Sometimes there's
chicken with pumkin and dasheen too;

I don't know what I would do
without Mammie's coo-coo and callaloo.

Sometimes there's
pelau, and on the side spicy manicou;

I don't know what I would do
without Mammie's coo-coo and callaloo.

Sometimes there's
poun plantain with curried cascadoo;

I don't know what I would do
without Mammie's coo-coo and callaloo.

Mmmmm, mmmmm I would like some now.
Would you like some too
of Mammie's coo-coo and callaloo?

Yeeeeeeesssssss!!!

I don't know what I would do
without Mammie's coo-coo and callaloo.

MY PRAYING MANTIS

I once had a mantis as a pet.
A praying mantis; you must not forget,

is the tiger of the insect world,
hungry, fierce and extremely bold;

and if you are an insect, keep away
should a mantis be lurking where you play.

Anyway, my mantis was my very best friend.
He sat on my shoulder, and I did defend

his insect's right to stay with me,
protect him from people's curiosity;

for they thought it very strange
the way his body was arranged:

For a start, his neck was very long,
and his heart-shaped head did not belong

to that thin neck and bulbous abdomen
or toothed arms as strong as ten,

wings which gave him speed in flight
when he attacked and with delight

grabbed a cockroach for his supper,
tore and ate it with his choppers.

However, one day, Phoebe, the neighbour's cat,
gobbled up my mantis and that was that.

Phoebe licked her lips, seemed satisfied
with a chewed-up mantis in her inside.

I suppose, for a mantis, the moral to this story
is, look out for cats or you'll be sorry.

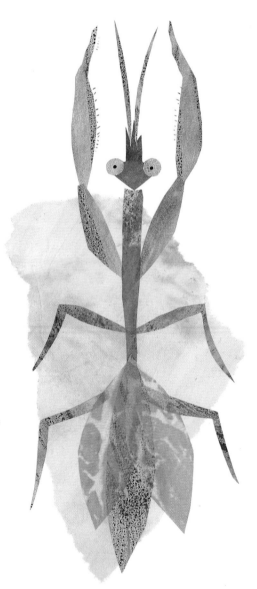

Nearly every day was a sunny day in the rural Jamaican village where I grew up. I spent most of my time outdoors. I had my own banana tree, my own pig, my own goat and a hen. When bananas from my tree were sold — or chicks from my hen or kids from my goat — the money was mine. From the age of about six I had jobs before and after school. Up early I would feed the chickens, get water at the standing pipe on the village road, collect firewood or run errands. I'd help to milk the goats or the cow. I'd fetch the horse, the donkey or the mule from some grassy patch where they'd been feeding all night. My village was near the sea and had a running stream. With my four brothers I went fishing from a cliff overhanging the sea and also went

James Berry

to catch shrimps in the stream. We swam in the sea. We picked young coconuts, chopped them open, drank the cooling water and scooped out the young, white and soft jelly coconut and ate it. We played cricket on the beach. We made all the things we played with: the bats, balls, kites, tops, wheels and so on. The first stories that really grabbed me were our Caribbean fun and horror folk tales, Anancy stories, which we told each other at home. As for reading, I had only my school texts, no other story-books or poems. When I came to England, at twenty-three, I was able to feast myself on a world of written poems and stories. My first poem was published when I was thirty-five and I have since written many books of stories and poems.

LETTER FROM YOUR SPECIAL-BIG-PUPPY-DOG

from Scribbled Notes Picked up by Owners and Rewritten because of bad grammar, bad spelling, bad writing

You know I'm so big
I'll soon become a person.
You know I want to know more
of all that you know. Yet
you leave the house, so, so often.
And not one quarrel between us.
Why don't you come home ten times
a day? Come, tell me the way
your boss is bad? See me sit,
listening, sad? And you know,

and I know, it's best
when you first come in.
You call my name. And O
I go starry-eyed on you,
can't stop wagging, jumping,
holding, licking your face,
saying, "D'you know – d'you know –
you're quite, quite a dish!"
Come home – come call my name –
every time thirty minutes pass.

LETTER FROM YOUR KITTEN-CAT-ALMOST-BIG-CAT

You tell me to clear up
the strings of wool off
the floor, just to see how
I slink out the door. But O
you're my mum. Fifty times
big to climb on. You stroke
my back from head to tail.
You tickle my furry throat,
letting my claws needle your side,
and my teeth nibble your hand
till I go quiet. I purr.
I purr like a poor boy
snoring, after gift of a dinner.

I leap into your lap only
to start everything over.

You see, I sign a letter myself PiG.
But O most of all
I want you to see
I want us to dig together,
wallow together and share
one bath. I want us to walk
together, all muddy and smart.
I want you to have
my work and my fun.

Isn't My Name Magical?

Nobody can see my name on me.
My name is inside
and all over me, unseen
like other people also keep it.
Isn't my name magical?

My name is mine only.
It tells I am individual,
the one special person it shakes
when I'm wanted.

Even if someone else answers
for me, my message hangs in air
haunting others, till it stops
with me, the right name.
Isn't your name and my name magic?

If I'm with hundreds of people
and my name gets called,
my sound switches me on to answer
like it was my human electricity.

My name echoes across playground,
it comes, it demands my attention.
I have to find out who calls,
who wants me for what.
My name gets blurted out in class,
it is terror, at a bad time,
because somebody is cross.

My name gets called in a whisper
I am happy, because
my name may have touched me
with a loving voice.
Isn't your name and my name magic?

Bye Now

Walk good
    Walk good
Noh mek macca go juk yu
Or cow go buk yu.
Noh mek dog bite yu
Or hungry go ketch yu, yah!

Noh mek sunhot turn yu dry.
Noh mek rain soak yu.
Noh mek tief tief yu.
Or stone go buck yu foot, yah!
    Walk good
      Walk good

Goodbye Now

Walk well
    Walk well
Don't let thorns run in you
Or let a cow butt you.
Don't let a dog bite you
Or hunger catch you, hear!

Don't let sun's heat turn you dry.
Don't let rain soak you.
Don't let a thief rob you
Or a stone bump your foot, hear!
    Walk well
      Walk well

Frank Collymore

Frank Collymore,
affectionately known as "Colly", died in 1980. But he lives on
in the memory of the Caribbean people for his unique
contribution to West Indian art and literature. A teacher by
profession he was also a painter, actor, writer, poet
and broadcaster, committed to freedom of expression and to
art in all its forms. From the early 1940s, right up until
1975 when he was eighty-two, he edited the literary magazine BIM.
There were times when the future of the magazine was uncertain,
but Colly kept it alive, almost single-handedly. Through his
teaching and letter-writing he was a friend and inspiration to
generations of Caribbean writers, giving them support and advice.
It is said that no letter to Colly ever went unanswered.
Collymore's poetry is light, humorous and full of the simple joys of life.
Above all it encapsulates the warmth and humanity that
he showed to others during his lifetime.

THE ZOBO BIRD

Do you think we skip,
Do you think we hop,
Do you think we flip,
Do you think we flop,
Do you think we trip
This fearful measure
And hop and hip
For personal pleasure?

O no, O no,
We are full of woe
From top to toe:
It's the dread Zobo,
    The Zobo bird.

He brings us bane,
He brings us blight,
He brings us pain
By day and night:
And so we must
Though it take all day
Dance or bust
Till he flies away.

Away, away!
O don't delay.
  Go, Zobo, go,
    O Zobo bird!

PHINNIPHIN

The tide is in,
   The tide is in,
      The Phinniphin
         Are out.

They love the sea,
   The salty sea,
      Of this there is
         No doubt.

O watch them flop
   And slip and slop
      With clumsy hop
         Right past

The sandy beach
   Until they reach
      The friendly sea
         At last.

But when the tide,
   The shifty tide
      Stays right outside
         The bar,

They can't go in
   The Phinniphin;
      The Phinniphin
         Cannot go in:
            They'd have to hop
            Too far.

THE SPIDER

I'm told that the spider
Has coiled up inside her
Enough silky material
To spin an aerial
One-way track
to the moon and back;
Whilst I
Cannot even catch a fly

Bibliographies

Opal Palmer Adisa,

Jamaican-born writer, has lived in California since 1979. Her published works are *Travelling Women*, a poetry collection with Devorah Major (Jukebox Press, Oakland, 1986); *Bake-Face and Other Guava Stories* (Kelsey Street Press, Berkeley, 1986) and *Pina, the Many-Eyed Fruit* (Julian Richardson Associate, San Francisco, 1985). Her poetry has appeared in many anthologies including *Caribbean Poetry Now* edited by Steward Brown (Hodder & Stoughton). Opal Palmer Adisa has written plays which have been produced in the Bay Area, and has taught at San Francisco State University. She is also a storyteller of Caribbean and African tales.

John Agard

was born in Guyana but has lived in Britain since 1977. He was attached to the Commonwealth Institute as a touring speaker for eight years during which time he visited some two thousand schools all across the UK talking about his Caribbean experience. His adult collection *Man to Pan* won the 1982 Casa de Las Americas Cuban Poetry Award. His other adult collections include *Mangoes and Bullets* and a book of love poems, *Lovelines for a Goat-born Lady*, published by Serpent's Tail. Among his many children's books are *I Din Do Nuttin*, *Laughter Is an Egg* and *The Emperor's Dan-Dan*, a picture book calypso retelling of *The Emperor's New Clothes*. He has also written plays for children.

James Berry

was born in a Jamaican coastal village and was among the early Caribbean settlers to Britain. He became involved with black people's cultural life from early on in the UK while steadily developing his writing, both for children and adults. He reads internationally, has broadcast on radio and television and conducted writers' workshops in schools over the years. Among his awards, his children's book *A Thief in the Village* won him the Smarties Prize for Children's Books and *When I Dance* the Signal Poetry Award. *Fractured Circles* and *Chain of Days* are among his adult poetry collections and he has also written a collection of stories for children, *Anancy Spiderman*. James won first prize in the Poetry Society's National Competition of 1981.

Valerie Bloom

was born in Clarendon, Jamaica, where she worked as a librarian before training as a teacher. She completed an Honours degree in English with African and Caribbean studies at the University of Kent, Canterbury, and later worked as Multicultural Arts Officer with North West Arts in Manchester. Her first book of poetry *Touch Mi, Tell Mi* was published in 1983 by Bogle L'Ouverture, and the revised edition in 1990. Her book of children's poems, *Duppy Jamboree*, was published by Cambridge University Press in 1992 and she has had poems published in several anthologies.

Dionne Brand

was born in Trinidad but now lives in Toronto, Canada. She has published six books of poetry – *Fore Day Morning*, *Earth Magic* (children's poetry), *Winter Epigrams*, *Primitive Offensive*, *Chronicles of the Hostile Sun* and *No Language is Neutral*, which was nominated for the 1990 Governor General's Awards. She has also co-authored a work of non-fiction, *Rivers Have Sources Trees Have Roots – Speaking of Racism*, and a book of short stories *Sans Souci and Other Stories*. Her latest book of non-fiction *No Burden to Carry, Narratives of Black Working Women in Ontario 1920s to 1950s* is a collection of oral histories.

David Campbell

is a songwriter, poet and singer. He was born and raised in Guyana, South America, but is now a Canadian citizen living in Vancouver, British Colombia. He has performed in concert and on radio and television in Britain, Europe and North America. David Campbell has written over one thousand songs, many of which have been recorded in albums such as *Through Arawak Eyes*, *Underneath the Blue Canadian Sky* and *Song*. His poems have appeared in his books of song lyrics. He has worked widely among the indigenous people of the Americas.

Faustin Charles

was born in Trinidad and came to Britain in 1962. He has had three collections of poetry published – *The Expatriate* in 1969, *Crab Track* in 1973 and *Days and Nights in the Magic Forest*. He has also written two novels and a book of West Indian folk-tales as well as books for children. He was a visiting lecturer for the Commonwealth Institute and has edited a collection of folk-tales from around the Caribbean – *Under the Storyteller's Spell*.

Frank Collymore

was born in Barbados in January 1893. He was a teacher and editor of the literary magazine BIM, to which he contributed numerous poems, short stories, plays, literary reviews and articles. He published several collections of poetry, including *Thirty Poems* (1944), *Beneath the Casuarinas* (1945), *Flotsam* (1948), *Collected Poems* (1959) and *Selected Poems* (1971). Frank Collymore died in July 1980. He is remembered by Barbadians as one of the island's greatest ever champions of literature and the arts.

John Lyons

is a Trinidadian-born painter and poet who has exhibited extensively, both nationally and internationally. He emigrated to England in 1959 and studied painting at Goldsmiths College, London and at the University of Newcastle-upon-Tyne. He won the Peterloo Afro-Caribbean/ Asian poetry prize on two occasions and was commended in the Poetry Society's National Poetry Competition. His first collection of poems, *Lure of the Cascadura*, was published by Bogle L'Ouverture in 1989. He is also one of four poets in a collection called *The Sun Rises in the North* (Smith/Doorstop Books, 1991).

Marc Matthews

is a Guyanese storyteller-poet-dramatist. His first collection published by Karnak House, *Guyana My Altar*, won the Guyana First Publication award in 1987. His most recent collection, published by People Tree Press, is titled A *Season of Sometimes*. He was an original member of the All-Ah-We team who, between 1973 and 1978, toured eleven Caribbean countries and made 160 performances. He has appeared in plays and feature films. He is now living in Guyana again after a number of years in the UK.

Pamela Mordecai

was born in Jamaica. Two of her children's books have been published: *Storypoems – a First Collection* (Ginn, 1987) and *Don't Ever Wake a Snake* (Sandberry Press, 1992). *Journey Poem*, a collection for adults, appeared in 1988. A Language Arts teacher, she has written or co-written some fifteen books for the Caribbean. In 1980 she was awarded the Institute of Jamaica's Tercentenary Medal for her writing. In 1993 her collection, *Ezra's Goldfish and Other Story-poems* won Jamaica's first Vic Reid Award for Children's Literature. She lives in Kingston where she and her husband, Martin, run Sandberry Press. They have three children.

Grace Nichols

was born in Guyana but has lived in Britain since 1977. Her publications for children include two collections of short stories: *Trust You Wriggly* and *Leslyn in London*, and a popular collection of poems, *Come On Into My Tropical Garden* (A&C Black). I *Is A Long Memoried Woman*, her first adult book of poems, won the 1983 Commonwealth Poetry Prize. Her other collections, *The Fat Black Woman's Poems* and *Lazy Thoughts of a Lazy Woman*, are both published by Virago along with her first novel, *Whole of a Morning Sky*. She has performed her poetry widely throughout Britain and abroad and has worked with both radio and television.

Telcine Turner

was born on New Providence Island, in the Bahamas. Her publications include a collection of poems for children, *Song of the Surreys* (Macmillan Caribbean, 1977); a full-length play, *Woman Take Two* (Vantage Press, New York, 1987); edited stories for children, *Once Below A Time* (Macmillan Caribbean, 1988), and edited stories and poems for schools, *Climbing Clouds* (Macmillan Caribbean 1988). She is married to the Bahamian artist, James O Rolle, and currently teaches at the College of the Bahamas.

Index of First Lines

KU-575-676

Outlaws

by Paul Thomas

Belitha Press

First published in 2002 in Great Britain by
Belitha Press,
an imprint of Chrysalis Children's Books plc.
64 Brewery Rd
London N7 9NT

ISBN 1 84138 4526

Printed by Midas, Hong Kong

Series editor: Veronica Ross
Editor: Honor Head
Series designer: Hayley Cove
Designer: Steve Wilson
Picture researcher: Diana Morris
Consultant: Hazel Mary Martell

Photographic credits
AKG, London: 7b Staatsbibliothek, SMPK Berlin; 42. Bridgeman Art Library: 12
Bodleian Library, Oxford; 16, 28 Private Collections. Corbis-Bettmann: 10, 19t, 40, 41;
43t Dorothea Lange; 43b. E.T. Archive: 36. Mary Evans Picture Library: 9b, 13b, 24
Bruce Castle Collection. Ronald Grant Archives: 5b Twentieth Century Fox. Hulton Getty
Collection Ltd: 6, 11b, 13t, 21b, 35b. The Kobal Collection: 5t Twentieth Century Fox.
The Mansell Collection: 15b. Peter Newark's Pictures: 4 Warner Brothers; 11t, 14, 17l,
17tr, 18, 19b, 20, 22, 23t, 23b, 25t, 25b, 26, 27t, 27b, 29t, 29b, 30, 31b, 32, 33t,
33b, 34, 35t, 37t, 37b, 38, 39b, 40b, 44t, 44b, 45t, 45b. North Wind Picture Archives:
7t, 8, 9t, 15t, 21t, 31t, 39t.

Words in **bold** appear in the glossary on page 46.

CONTENTS

INTRODUCTION

There are many different reasons why people throughout history have turned to a life of crime and become outlaws. For some it was the only way they could fight injustice. For others, it was a quick way to become rich and famous.

Glamour and fame

Outlaws were usually ruthless and violent people who terrorized and threatened others. But over the years, television and films have glamorized many outlaws. Living outside the law is often seen as exciting, daring and dangerous. Many films about Wild West outlaws, such as Jesse James and Billy the Kid, show them as daring heroes rather than criminals.

Later, modern-day outlaws became known as gangsters. Bonnie and Clyde were two of the best-known gangsters of all time. Although they killed many people and died violently, they are shown as a good-looking, glamorous couple in the 1967 film starring Faye Dunaway and Warren Beatty.

Worldwide crime

In England there were different sorts of outlaws. During the eighteenth century highwaymen held up people on horseback or in coaches. Perhaps the most famous highwayman is Dick Turpin.

Earlier, there were many outlaws of the seas, or pirates as they were known, and the most feared and ruthless of these was Blackbeard. In Australia, outlaws were called bushrangers and were mostly escaped convicts. In his famous iron suit and helmet, Ned Kelly became the best-known outlaw from this part of the world.

Faye Dunaway and Warren Beatty in the 1967 film *Bonnie and Clyde*.

Dangerous women

Some of the most fierce and daring outlaws in history were women. Belle Starr was thought to be the toughest cowgirl in the Wild West. Mary Read and Anne Bonny were said to be two of the bravest pirates on the high seas.

Fighting for a cause

Not all outlaws chose their way of life just to become rich or for their own gain. Robin Hood in England and William Tell in Switzerland put themselves outside the law in order to fight injustice and not for personal gain.

Above, Henry Fonda leaping into action in the film *Jesse James*.

Below, Jean Peters played *Anne of the Indies*, a film about Anne Bonny, a fierce female pirate.

WILLIAM TELL

Late thirteenth century

The **legend** of William Tell is about the struggles of the people of Switzerland to overcome the harsh rule of the Austrians. Tell's bravery and courage inspired others to fight.

William Tell was born into a **peasant** family in the **canton** of Uri. At the time of his birth Switzerland was made up of a group of individual cantons, or communities. Along with the cantons of Schwyz (from which the name Switzerland comes) and Unterwalden, Uri was one of the main areas of peasant **resistance** against the hated and cruel Austrians.

Austrian rule

In 1273 Rudolf of Hapsburg became ruler of Germany and Switzerland. The Swiss agreed to accept his rule because he respected their laws. After Rudolf's death in 1291 his grandson, Albert of Austria, took over. Albert sent **governors** to Switzerland to make sure the Swiss people obeyed Austrian rule.

These governors were often greedy and ruthless. They demanded that the peasants hand over their cattle and other property to them, and forced the people to pay large taxes.

William Tell symbolized Switzerland's struggle for political freedom. He is also well-known for his skill with a crossbow.

Gessler's cap

In 1307 Gessler, the brutal Austrian governor of Uri, ordered the townspeople to bow to a cap hung in the square at Altdorf as a sign of respect for the Austrian emperor. Tell refused to bow to the cap. Gessler, who had heard that Tell was an expert with the crossbow, demanded an unusual and cruel punishment.

Shooting the apple

An apple was placed on the head of William Tell's son, and Tell was ordered to shoot it off with an arrow fired from his crossbow. William Tell drew two arrows from his quiver. The little boy was so far away the apple was almost invisible, but Tell successfully shot the apple in two without harming his son. Gessler asked Tell why he had drawn two arrows from his quiver. William Tell replied that if he had killed his son he would have killed Gessler.

William Tell was ordered to shoot an apple off his son's head. His son was so far away, it was thought he would miss the apple and kill his son.

Switzerland

Switzerland is best known for its range of high mountains called the Swiss Alps and its picture-book beauty. It is also known as a peaceful country which has not been involved in a war since 1815. It stayed neutral during the two World Wars earlier this century. Many international organizations, such as the **Red Cross**, are based in Switzerland.

A great storm

Gessler called William Tell a **traitor** and an **assassin**, and ordered his arrest. Tell was captured and taken on board a boat sailing for Gessler's **fortress** where there was a prison. But as they crossed the great lake, a violent storm arose and the boat was unable to pull into the shore. Gessler was terrified of drowning and he agreed to free Tell, who was known for his sailing skills. Tell said he would bring the boat safely to shore. But he tricked the crew and leapt overboard with his crossbow.

Death of Gessler

Tell was so afraid that Gessler would capture and torture his family that he vowed to kill him. He did not have to wait long for an opportunity to carry out his promise. Gessler and his crew survived the storm. As they were making their way to the fortress, they were ambushed by Tell who shot Gessler with his crossbow.

Liberation of Switzerland

Tell escaped and returned to Uri where he organized the Swiss rebels into a powerful fighting force. His aim was to drive the Austrians out of Switzerland. In 1315, the Swiss rebels faced the Austrian army at the Battle of Morganten. The Austrians were better equipped, but the Swiss put up a fierce fight and won. This battle has become one of the most important in Swiss history.

William Tell escaped from Gessler's boat by leaping ashore during a storm.

The crossbow

William Tell is known for his skill with the crossbow. This was originally a **medieval** weapon that could fire small arrows with great force. A crossbow was usually made up of a metal bow that was fixed to the end of a wooden handle. There was a groove inside the handle which held the arrow, a trigger to release it and a crank for drawing the bow string tight.

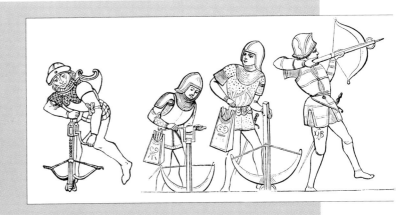

A free country

The victory at Morganten encouraged other cantons like Lucerne, Zurich and Berne to join the rebellion. Eventually the cantons joined together to create a **confederation** and became known as The Confederation of Switzerland, an independent and free country.

Man or myth?

Nothing is known about William Tell after the Battle of Morganten although some books say he died in a flood in 1350. Many people believe that he is just a popular **legend**. But for the Swiss people, William Tell is a national hero who symbolizes their struggle for freedom.

The Swiss beating the Austrians at the Battle of Morganten.

ROBIN HOOD

Early fourteenth century

The most famous outlaw of all time is Robin Hood, and yet he is also the one we know least about. We do not even know if he really existed or if he is just a mythical figure whose story has grown over the centuries.

The story of Robin Hood's life was passed down from one generation to another through songs and tales, so it is difficult to know how much of the **legend** is true. It is thought that the adventures of Robin Hood are based on stories of lots of different outlaws mixed up together. One story claims that Robin lived in Sherwood Forest, in Nottinghamshire, in the twelfth century. Another story says that Robin Hood was the Earl of Huntingdon, Robert Fitzooth, who was outlawed for his part in a rebellion in 1265.

The real Robin Hood?

Records show that a person named Robert Hood was born in 1290 in Wakefield, Yorkshire. He may have become the famous outlaw because at that time Robin was a popular nickname for people called Robert. In the legend, Robin Hood married Maid Marian. Records show that Robert Hood's wife was called Matilda, which could have become Marian.

Robin Hood is mentioned in the poem *Piers Ploughman*, written in 1377.

Rebel and outlaw

In 1322 Robin's landlord, the Earl of Lancaster, ordered his **tenants** to rebel against King Edward II. A tenant had to obey, and Robin followed the Earl into battle as an archer. The revolt was soon crushed, and Lancaster was tried for treason and beheaded.

Robin Hood and his men robbing the Bishop of Hereford who has been tied to a tree.

Band of Merry Men

Robin's followers are as much a part of the legend as Robin Hood himself. Little John, who was given his nickname because he was so big and strong, was one of the first members of Robin Hood's band of outlaws. Friar Tuck, shown here on the donkey, is another well-known member of the band. He was a jolly monk who enjoyed his food and good company.

Escape to the forest

All the Earl's possessions were taken by the king and his followers were outlawed. Robin could not return home, so he fled into Barnsdale Forest in Yorkshire which was joined to Nottinghamshire's Sherwood Forest. The two forests covered a huge area of land and made an ideal hiding place.

A legend is born

A road ran through the forests joining London and the north. Robbers made rich pickings from the travellers who used it. And Robin Hood was no exception. According to legend, Robin Hood robbed the rich to give to the poor. Tales of how he could outwit the king's men and humiliate the wealthy and influential made him very popular with the poor. His skill as an archer and stories about his faithful band of followers soon became part of the legend.

A private hunting ground

The forest would have been very different from the forest we know today. It was the private hunting ground of the lords of the manor or the king, and contained lots of game, including deer. Much of the forest would have been densely wooded, but there would also have been clearings where Robin and his men could set up camp.

The king's plan

In 1323 King Edward II travelled to the north of England to make sure the rebellion of the previous year was over and to capture Robin Hood. He planned to disguise himself and his knights as monks and ride into Sherwood Forest in the hope that Robin and his men would try to rob him.

A royal pardon

The plan worked and the king and his men were stopped by the outlaws who demanded money. The king said he had £40 so Robin took £20 and gave the rest back. Edward then produced the royal **seal** on his finger. The outlaws knelt down in front of the seal and swore their **allegiance** to the king. Edward said he would **pardon** all the outlaws if they agreed to come to his court and serve him. They all agreed.

Records show Robin Hood's name in the household accounts of Edward II in 1324, but after that his name vanishes. It was said that he could not settle to live in the service of the king and returned to the forest.

King Edward II, who pardoned Robin Hood and his men, ruled England for 20 years with his wife, Queen Isabella of France.

Rob Roy

Rob Roy Macgregor, the Robin Hood of Scotland, spent his life in the Scottish Highlands. He was an excellent swordsman and had a reputation for being fearless. In 1691 he joined the **Jacobites** who were supporters of the **exiled** king, James II. The Jacobite rising failed in 1716 and Rob became an outlaw. His reputation as a hero of the people spread across Scotland. He was captured and jailed in Newgate Prison in London in 1722, but he was pardoned in 1727. He died seven years later. His fame grew when Sir Walter Scott's novel, *Rob Roy*, was published in 1818.

Deathbed shot

Robin's adventures in the forests continued until 1346, when he is thought to have died at Kirklees **Priory** near Leeds after a long illness. Legend says that on his deathbed, he shot an arrow from the window of his room. Robin Hood asked to be buried where the arrow fell.

The spot said to be his grave can still be seen near the priory. Many stories and songs about Robin Hood have been handed down from generation to generation and have helped to turn him into the legend we know today. One of these is the story *Ivanhoe* by Sir Walter Scott.

Robin Hood shot his last arrow when he was dying. He was buried on the spot where the arrow landed.

BLACKBEARD

1680–1718

Many sailors turned to piracy at the end of the war of the **Spanish Succession**. Among these was one of the most feared and hated pirates of all time, Blackbeard.

Mystery surrounds the beginnings of Blackbeard's life. It is not certain whether he was born in Bristol, England or in Jamaica, in about 1680. Even the spelling of his real name is unclear – it could have been Edward Teach, Tatch or Thatch. Blackbeard went to the West Indies in 1701 to fight for England as a **privateer**, but he soon turned to piracy.

In 1713 Blackbeard captured a French merchant ship. He fitted out the ship with forty large cannons and renamed her *Queen Anne's Revenge*.

Demon of the seas

Teach was nicknamed Blackbeard because of his appearance, which struck terror into his victims. His thick black beard was long and plaited and tied with ribbons. He was well over 1.8 metres tall, and when he went into a fight he would wear a sling over his shoulders with six pistols tucked into it. He swooped down on his victims with a wild and fierce look in his eyes.

When he went into battle, Blackbeard would light slow-burning fuses under his hat. Black smoke curled around his head making him look like a demon.

A pirate's life

Most pirates were desperate robbers and killers on the run from the law. But some were honest seamen who were forced into piracy when their ships were captured. The pirate captain was elected by the crew, but he only had command when the ship was about to attack. After that, every man could do as he pleased. **Plunder** was shared out fairly among the crew and if a pirate suffered an injury during a fight, he was given extra payment. Pirates drank huge amounts of alcohol, and a mixture of rum and gunpowder was a favourite cocktail. Most pirates died fighting or on the gallows.

Shipwreck!

Blackbeard and his crew then decided to sail further north to Topsail Inlet in North Carolina. It was here that two of his ships, including the *Queen Anne's Revenge*, were wrecked. Some of his crew went to join other pirate ships, but Blackbeard and about 30 men decided to approach the king of England, George l, and beg for mercy.

The coast of America

By 1717 Blackbeard's fearsome reputation was established. With his crew of ruthless pirates he sailed through the West Indies, and north along the American coast, capturing and plundering many ships. In 1718 Blackbeard **blockaded** Charleston harbour in South Carolina. He sent some of his men into the town to demand a chest full of gold and jewels. The residents knew that Blackbeard would attack if they didn't pay up.

A drawing of an English privateer ship capturing a **frigate**. Many privateers, such as Blackbeard, became pirates.

Blackbeard raided ships sailing along the American coast. He was ruthless and fought fiercely.

Secret plans

The pirates wanted a royal pardon, which meant they would not be hanged. But Blackbeard had his own secret plan. He had already set up a business partnership with the **governor** of North Carolina, Charles Eden. Blackbeard agreed to share his booty with Eden in exchange for a royal pardon. This was easy for the governor to arrange, and so Blackbeard walked away a free man, while his crew members were hanged in Virginia.

But Blackbeard soon became bored with his law-abiding life, and he started to run out of money. It was not long before he gave up life on dry land, and went back to piracy.

The people seek revenge

Blackbeard carried on robbing ships and demanding money from the people of North Carolina. He also blocked the river and demanded money from any vessel that used it.

Eventually the local people decided they had to do something about Blackbeard. They knew they could not go to Eden, their own governor. Instead they went to the governor of the neighbouring state of Virginia, Alexander Spotswood, who wanted to protect Virginia's trade from the pirates.

Help at last

Spotswood planned to ambush Blackbeard's ships and hired Captain Robert Maynard to hunt him down. On 22 November 1718 Captain Maynard set sail with two ships, **HMS** *Pearl* and *HMS Lyme*, in search of Blackbeard. They caught up with his ship in the Ocracoke Inlet.

The pirate flags

Many pirates sailed under a black flag with a white skull and crossbones on it. This was called the Jolly Roger. Some pirates made up their own version of the Jolly Roger. Blackbeard's flag had a black background with the picture of a white skeleton holding an hourglass in one hand and an arrow striking at a bleeding heart in the other. These pictures warned his victims that time was running out.

When Blackbeard was finally killed his head was cut off and fixed to the bow of his ship to prove to people that he was really dead.

The last fight

As they came alongside the pirate vessel, Maynard's ships hoisted the **king's flag**. Blackbeard fired his cannons at them. Maynard's ships did not have any big guns, but they fired back with small firearms. The pirate ship ran aground and sailors and pirates boarded each other's ships to fight.

Maynard and Blackbeard fought each other face to face with pistols and swords. Blackbeard was shot five times with a pistol and received 20 **cutlass** wounds before he fell to the deck, dead.

The other pirates fought on until only six remained alive, all wounded. Maynard cut off Blackbeard's head and hung it from a bar over the **bow** of his ship. It is said that the headless corpse swam around the ship three times before sinking.

MARY READ

1690–1720

Mary Read is one of the most famous female pirates in history. She dressed like a man and fought as hard as any of the male pirates.

Disguised as a man, Mary Read roamed the seas as a fierce and bloody pirate. She could use a sword and a pistol as well as any male pirate.

Mary Read was born in England in 1690. Her father was a sea captain who left his family soon after Mary was born. Read's mother brought her daughter up as a boy. Some say this is because she wanted an inheritance from her wealthy mother-in-law who would be more likely to leave money to a boy. Others say it is because she was deeply affected by the recent death of a baby son.

In search of adventure

When her grandmother died, Read continued to dress as a boy. When she was 13, she was sent to work for a French lady as a **footboy**. But Read was outgoing and restless, and eager for some excitement in her life. She soon became bored with domestic service and decided to go in search of adventure.

She signed up to work on board a warship as a powder-monkey. These were boys who made sure the **ammunition** or gunpowder for the big cannons was always ready. No one guessed that she was really a girl in disguise.

Mary Read was disguised as a man when her pirate ship was captured by another. She was taken prisoner because she was the only English 'man' on board.

A short marriage

Read stayed on board the warship for six years until she deserted. She joined a **foot regiment** in Flanders and went to fight the French. It was during this time that she fell in love with one of the officers. Read took a great risk and revealed her true identity to him. Before long the couple were married. They left the army to open a tavern near Breda in Holland.

In disguise again

Read's husband died suddenly and the tavern started to lose money. To avoid a life of poverty, Read once again disguised herself as a man and joined up with another foot regiment. But she soon deserted the regiment for a ship bound for the West Indies. Read's ship was captured by English pirates and, as the only English 'man' on board, they took her with them. She stayed with the pirates until 1717 when George I of England issued a **pardon** for any pirates who would leave the trade.

Anne Bonny

Anne Bonny, shown here (left) with Mary Read, was born in Ireland in 1700 and raised in Charleston, South Carolina. She became a pirate when she met her pirate husband, James Bonny. Several years later she ran off with the pirate Calico Jack. They sailed the seas off Cuba and Haiti attacking Spanish ships. After her trial and release, Bonny returned to Charleston.

Life on land

Read took advantage of the offer of a pardon and returned to life on land. But she was soon back in disguise and went to join an outfit of **privateers** who were preying on Spanish ships. In 1718, Read's ship was captured by a pirate ship, commanded by Captain Jack Rackham, known as Calico Jack.

Read and Bonny

With Calico Jack was his companion Anne Bonny, who was also disguised as a man. Mary Read and Anne Bonny became close friends, and Read confessed to Bonny that she was a woman. Soon after this Read fell in love with Peter Hines, an Englishman who was serving on board. Read's love for him was so strong that she arranged to take his place in a duel and successfully fought it for him.

Too drunk to fight

In 1720, Captain Rackham's ship was captured off the coast of Jamaica by a government ship. Rackham and his men had been drinking heavily and were too drunk to fight. They remained below deck, still drinking, while Read and Bonny, armed with swords and pistols, tried to fight off the government men.

Mary Read fought a duel on behalf of her lover, Peter Hines. Read was a much better swordsman than Hines and had a greater chance of winning.

The pirate queen

Ching Yih Saoa sailed the China Seas at the beginning of the nineteenth century. She ran a fleet of nearly 2000 junks, Chinese ships (right), crewed by over 70 000 male and female pirates. She made a fortune by **plundering** merchant ships, raiding towns and taking hundreds of prisoners for ransom. The Chinese government tried to capture her many times, but they always failed. They eventually offered her a pardon which she accepted, and settled down to a life of luxury.

Mary Read visited Calico Jack in prison in Jamaica before he was hanged for piracy. Read was freed because she was pregnant.

Capture and trial

Read and Bonny put up a fierce fight, but they were soon disarmed. They were arrested, together with Rackham and the rest of the crew, and sent to be tried for piracy. They were taken to St Jago de la Vega in Jamaica. Jack Rackham and several of his crew were found guilty and sentenced to death by hanging. This was the usual punishment for acts of piracy.

Witnesses were called who said Read had taken part in acts of piracy around Jamaica. They also said that she wore men's clothes and was able to use a pistol and a sword as well as any man.

Death or prison?

Read and Bonny were both found guilty of piracy but claimed they were pregnant by saying, 'My lord, we plead our bellies'. They were examined and were not given the death penalty because they were due to give birth. Read was not to enjoy her reprieve for long. Just a few months later she died of a fever.

DICK TURPIN

1705–1739

Highway robbery thrived in Britain in the seventeenth and eighteenth centuries when roads were deserted, coach travel slow and the law weak. There were many highwaymen but none as famous as Dick Turpin.

Turpin was born on 25 September 1705 at the Ben Inn in the village of Hempstead, Essex. The inn was owned by his father, who was an ex-butcher. At the age of 16 Turpin became an apprentice to a London butcher. The move to the big city gave him a taste for the richer things in life which he was unable to afford as a butcher. So at night Turpin started a second career as a footpad, a highwayman on foot. This made him enough money to be able to return to Essex, get married, and set up his own butcher's shop.

The Essex Gang

But the business was not very successful, and Dick Turpin soon returned to a life of crime to pay for his extravagant lifestyle. He joined a notorious gang of burglars known as the Essex Gang. The members of the gang were among the most wanted men in the London area.

Legend says that Dick Turpin rode from London to York to escape capture in just 12 hours. His horse, Black Bess, died of exhaustion just before they reached York.

Dick Turpin shooting the keeper who discovered his hideout in Epping Forest. After this a reward of £200 was offered for Turpin's capture.

Through the window

The gang poached deer and broke into houses, threatening and torturing the people who lived there before escaping with whatever they could. A £100 reward was offered for their capture. The authorities eventually caught up with the gang, but Turpin escaped by jumping out of a window. Two other members of the gang were arrested, tried and hanged.

Dog eat dog

Turpin decided to return to highway robbery, but this time on horseback. He set up his hideout in a cave in Epping Forest. In 1736 Turpin attempted to rob a smartly dressed rider on the Cambridge Road. His intended victim burst into laughter and cried, 'What! Dog eat dog?' The other man was Tom King, one of the most famous highwaymen of the day and known as the gentleman highwayman. Turpin and King became partners. King taught Turpin that he would be more successful if he treated his victims with a little courtesy.

Tyburn gallows

Tyburn gallows, also known as the Tyburn Tree, was the main place of execution by hanging from 1300 to 1783. It was near London's Marble Arch, and a plaque marks the spot. A hanging was a popular social event. High prices were paid for the best seats at the gallows. The prisoner was taken to the gallows on the back of a horse-drawn cart. This journey was like a royal procession, with the crowds cheering and throwing flowers at the prisoner.

Dick Turpin may have accidentally shot Tom King while trying to save him from being arrested.

Fatal chase

The partnership only lasted a year. Turpin and King had stolen a famous racehorse called White Stockings, which was easily recognized by many people. One evening Turpin was seen riding through the streets of London on the horse. He was reported and the authorities set up a chase. As they raced after him, Turpin saw King being arrested and went to help him. In the chaos that followed, King was shot dead. Some say he was shot by the authorities, other reports say that he was accidentally shot by Turpin who then managed to escape.

A new identity

Dick Turpin moved north and set himself up in Yorkshire as a country gentleman called John Palmer. Turpin made money by stealing sheep and horses. In 1739, after a particularly wild night, he began firing off his pistols in the street. Annoyed neighbours reported him, and he ended up in jail while the local authorities investigated his recent activities.

Highwaymen

Many highwaymen adopted amusing disguises when robbing travellers. James Collet disguised himself as a bishop, while Thomas Sympson wore women's clothes. One highwayman, Jonathan Simpson, wore ice skates and held up people on the frozen River Thames. But the popular image of a highwayman is of a man on horseback, pointing a pistol, wearing a black eye mask and cloak, and making the command, 'Stand and deliver. Your money or your life.'

All is revealed

Under the **alias** John Palmer, Turpin wrote to his family asking them to come forward to help him clear his name. Unfortunately for Turpin, the postmaster was his old schoolteacher who had taught him to read and write. Amazingly, after so many years, the teacher recognized his pupil's handwriting and reported his discovery of the letter to the authorities.

Going in style

John Palmer was identified as Dick Turpin and arrested. He admitted everything, was tried at York, and sentenced to be hanged. On the morning of 7 April 1739 Turpin was taken to the gallows on what is now York racecourse. He bowed and waved to all the spectators who had come to see England's most famous highwayman die. **Legend** has it that when he arrived at the gallows he chatted in a friendly manner with the hangman. He then stood with his head high, the noose around his neck, and hurled himself from the scaffold to ensure a quick death.

Illustration for
The Ballad of Dick Turpin
showing him wearing a typical
highwayman's hat and mask.

BELLE STARR

1846–1889

Belle Starr was a well-educated, intelligent woman who rode out in velvet and feathers. She was also one of the most fierce and reckless outlaws in the American west.

Belle Starr was born Myra Belle Shirley, on 5 February 1846 in Missouri. Belle came from a wealthy family. Her father, John Shirley, was a businessman from Virginia who bought a **homestead** in Missouri to make a new life for himself and his family.

Bad company

When she was eight Belle went to Carthage Female Academy, which was one of the finest schools in the area. This peaceful life continued until a local war broke out on the borders of Kansas and Missouri, and gangs set fire to John Shirley's ranch. He decided to move his family away from the trouble, and they left for Texas. Belle was 15 years old.

The family settled in a small town called Scyene, east of Dallas. By the time Belle was 18 it was obvious to most people who knew her that she preferred the company of gangsters and thieves.

Belle Starr was nicknamed the Bandit Queen of Oklahoma. She joined up with many other outlaws and ran a hideout for wanted criminals.

Women outlaws

Belle Starr was not the only female outlaw in the American west. Cattle Annie McDougal (above left) and Little Britches (Jennie) Metcalf (above right), started their careers by **bootlegging** whisky before switching to rustling cattle. Rose Dunn, nicknamed the Rose of Cimarron, became one of the best horse-thieves in the west.

Encountering outlaws

Belle's first encounter with outlaws was with the handsome Cole Younger, who was part of the Jesse James Gang. Belle sheltered Younger when he was on the run after robbing a bank. They had a child, Pearl, but Cole Younger abandoned Belle and their daughter.

Belle met another outlaw, Jim Reed, and they soon set up a partnership. They moved to California where their son was born, but returned to Texas in 1869. They made a living **rustling** horses and robbing banks and trains.

Bandit Queen

Belle called herself the Bandit Queen. She always insisted on riding sidesaddle and she wore velvet dresses and feathers, as well as a holster with pistols. When Jim Reed was killed in 1874, Belle decided to leave her children with her mother and rode out of town seeking adventure and a new partner.

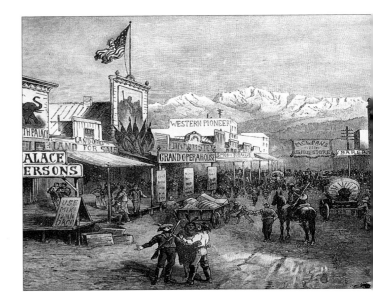

An illustration of a Wild West town as it would have been in Belle Starr's time. It shows familiar sights such as an opera house and a grocery store.

Hideout ranch

In 1880 Belle married a **Native American**, a tall, slim Cherokee called Sam Starr. They led a gang which stole cattle and horses. Their home was a log cabin near Fort Smith in Arkansas, which become well-known as a hideout for some of the most wanted outlaws of the day. Belle was thought to be the mastermind behind the gang's activities.

Law expert

Belle Starr and her gang were charged many times with horse-stealing and other criminal acts. But unlike most of her fellow outlaws, Belle was educated and she understood the law. She was smart enough to get many of the cases against her dismissed due to lack of evidence. In 1883 Belle and Sam Starr were convicted of horse-stealing and imprisoned. But as soon as they were released from jail they went back to their life of crime.

Cowgirls and the rodeo

Many women in the American west learned the same skills as cowboys. Cowgirls doing trick riding, roping and bronco riding became very popular at rodeo shows. One of the best known cowgirls was Lucille Mulhall. She could catch eight horses at a time with one throw of her lasso. Calamity Jane (right) joined Buffalo Bill's Wild West show and demonstrated her riding and sharpshooting skills. Annie Oakley was another top attraction in Buffalo Bill's show. She could shoot a cigarette from her husband's lips, dimes from his fingers, and hit a target behind her using a hand mirror.

This painting, called *Rustlers* by William H D Koerner, shows outlaws riding in to steal cattle and horses. Starr and her partners were expert cattle rustlers.

The unknown killer

Belle told Jim that the authorities had no case against him and that he should give himself up and plead not guilty. She planned to handle his case in court. On 3 February 1889 Belle Starr and Jim July set out for Fort Smith. The following morning Jim was seen going on alone. Later, Belle was found dying in the dust, having been shot in the back.

The identity of Belle Starr's killer has never been discovered. Some people said the murderer was Jim July because Starr had decided not to help him. It was even thought it could have been her son, Edward, with whom she had a stormy relationship, but the truth will never be known.

Belle Starr photographed with one of her many outlaw partners, a Native American called Blue Duck.

A price on her head

The Starrs were now so notorious that the US Government offered $10 000 in gold coins for information leading to their arrest. Although this was a huge amount of money in those days, no one came forward with evidence that could be used to prosecute the pair.

A new partner

Sam Starr was killed in a gunfight with a deputy sheriff in 1886. Belle mourned his death, but she soon took up with another outlaw. Like Sam, Jim July was a Native American, a Creek Indian. They met when Jim, who was wanted for robbery, was hiding out at Starr's cabin.

JESSE JAMES

1847–1882

A photograph of Jesse James aged 17 taken during the American Civil War.

Jesse James came from a respectable religious family. He grew up during the **American Civil War** and the railway boom, both of which made a big impact on his life, but in different ways.

James' father was a Baptist preacher who set up a Baptist school in Clay County, Missouri, where James was born. He had a brother, Frank, and a sister, Susan. When Jesse was only three years old his father left for California to try and find gold. He was only there for a few weeks before he died of an unknown illness.

Guerrilla gangs

James' mother remarried a wealthy man and had four more children. The family were slave owners, and when the American Civil War began in 1861 they sided with the south. The southern states supported slavery, while the northern states wanted to see slavery abolished.

In the summer of 1863, when Jesse was 16, his family was attacked by anti-slavery supporters. His stepfather was nearly hanged and Jesse was badly beaten. As a result, Jesse joined a **guerrilla** group fighting against the north. He learned how to fight and how to shoot.

The great gold rush

There have been many gold rushes in American history, but the most famous was in 1849 when gold was discovered at Sutter's Mill on the American River, California. It caused the largest migration of people over the longest distances in the briefest span of time in the history of the world. California's population grew from 14 000 in 1848 to 380 000 in 1860. People came from China, Australia and Europe.

End of the war

Two years later the Civil War ended. Jesse and his brother, Frank, who had also fought in the Civil War, found it difficult to settle into a routine life after the excitement of the war years. They met up with some other ex-guerrillas, including Jim and Cole Younger, who were also bored with the peace and the thought of a lifetime spent as farmers.

The James-Younger Gang

The Younger brothers and the James brothers decided to escape from everyday life and to look for excitement outside the law. Together they formed a ruthless gang led by Jesse James. Over the next 16 years the gang brutally robbed banks and trains, killing many innocent staff and bystanders.

Cole Younger

Bob Younger (rear)

Jesse James

Frank James

Jesse James and his brother Frank photographed with the Younger brothers. Together they formed one of the most violent and ruthless gangs in the American west.

Train robbers

Railway building had boomed in America since the days of the Civil War. Railways stretched across the country, carrying valuable cargo such as gold and money, as well as passengers. Many gangs had already begun to realize that trains were a good source of loot, and the James gang was no exception. They carried out a daring train robbery in their home state of Missouri at Gad's Hill. They also continued to rob banks, escaping with large sums of money.

Pinkerton detectives

In 1871 banking officials hired the Pinkerton National Detective Agency to try and capture Jesse James. A Pinkerton agent was killed when sent out to arrest the James brothers. Four years later a bomb was thrown into their mother's house, causing her to lose an arm, and killing their stepbrother. It was believed to have been thrown by Pinkerton men. Public sympathy turned in Jesse's favour and the detectives were called off.

Robin Hood of the west

The gang had many supporters among ordinary people who disliked the banks. This was because banks charged high interest rates on borrowed money. Jesse's supporters were very pleased to see the banks and railroads robbed of their profits, and Jesse James gained a reputation as a modern-day Robin Hood. Dime novels and boys' comics all made up stories about Jesse James and his exciting adventures.

Legend says that Jesse would steal only from passengers from the northern states when he robbed trains. He said the northerners had forced him into a life of crime, so only northerners should pay. But in reality it was mainly southerners who were terrorized and killed by his gang.

This illustration from the *The Police Gazette* shows Jesse James and his gang robbing a train in 1881. They stole cargo and forced passengers to hand over their valuables.

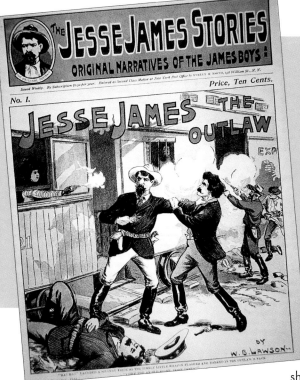

Dime novels

During Jesse James' life and after he was killed, his adventures were written about in many books, such as *The Jesse James Stories*. These were called dime novels because they only cost a dime, or 10 cents. They were the idea of Erastus Beadle who launched the series in June 1860. They brought the excitement of the west to readers all over America. Robert Leroy Parker was one person who enjoyed dime novels. He was later known as Butch Cassidy.

Robert Ford, a new member of Jesse's gang, shot him in the back of the head.

Jesse betrayed

In 1881, Jesse robbed a train in Missouri, killing the conductor and a passenger. This caused public outrage and led to a reward of $10 000 for his capture, dead or alive. Some time later, two new gang members, Charles and Robert Ford, were staying with Jesse prior to a bank robbery planned for the next day. After finishing his breakfast, Jesse reached up to straighten a picture. Robert Ford pulled out his gun, aimed at Jesse and shot him in the back of the head. He later claimed the reward.

Jesse's brother, Frank, gave himself up in exchange for being **pardoned** for most of his crimes. He served two years in prison and was released in 1885. Frank was to live for another 30 years as a law abiding farmer until his death in 1915.

NED KELLY

1855–1880

In Australia outlaws were called bushrangers because they hid in the vast bush. During the nineteenth century there were many bushrangers, the best-known being Ned Kelly.

During the nineteenth century many criminals were sent to penal colonies in Australia from England and Ireland. Ned Kelly's father was transported to Australia from Belfast, Ireland, for stealing pigs. The Kellys decided to stay in Australia and settled in the state of Victoria.

Ned Kelly's father died when Ned was 11 years old. This made Ned, the eldest of seven children, the man of the family. The Kellys were constantly in trouble with the police for all sorts of petty crimes, and Ned Kelly grew up believing that the authorities were the enemy.

A bad start

At the age of 15, Ned Kelly was arrested for taking part in a robbery. But there was no evidence to link him to the robbery, and he was allowed to go. Six months later he was again arrested, this time on a charge of assaulting a police officer. In 1871 he was arrested again and this time he was jailed for three years.

This photograph was taken of Ned Kelly just a few days before his execution in 1880. He was captured in a spectacular shoot-out.

The Kelly Gang with Ned, holding the shotgun, and his brother Dan in the middle.

The Kelly Gang

In April 1878 a policeman went to the Kelly household to arrest Ned's brother, Dan. Their mother hit the policeman over the head with a spade! Although the policeman was not seriously hurt, she was sentenced to three years in prison while her sons went on the run. Ned and Dan Kelly were joined by two other outlaws and formed the Kelly Gang. In October 1878 two police search parties set out to hunt the Kelly Gang. They came upon the gang at Stringybark Creek and, in the gunfight that followed, three policemen were shot and killed.

Penal colonies

Penal colonies were prisons where convicts from Britain were sent to help ease the overcrowding in British jails. The convicts were transported in special ships like the one shown here. The first penal colony was set up in what is now the city of Sydney by Captain Arthur Phillip who landed in Australia on 26 January 1788. Convicts were poorly housed, clothed and fed. They often worked in chain gangs, and were severely punished for the smallest offence. In the 1800s **immigrants** began to set up farms in Australia, and convicts were used as farm workers.

Showing off

The people of the state of Victoria were shocked at the news. A reward of £1000 was offered for Kelly's arrest, and an army of police scoured the bush to try to find him. But instead of lying low, the Kelly Gang seemed to be making fun of the police. On 9 December 1878, the Kelly Gang robbed a bank in Euroa, Victoria. Instead of making a quick escape, Kelly insisted on taking the bewildered bank manager, his family and two servants on a picnic where he showed off his riding skills. The police did not catch them. It seemed the Kelly Gang was always one step ahead.

Ned Kelly's suit of armour

Ned Kelly's armour was made out of plough shares, the metal blades on a plough that turn the soil. They were melted and shaped to fit. The suit consisted of four pieces: a massive square helmet with a slit for the eyes, a front part which covered his chest and stomach, a back piece and an apron which covered his thighs. His arms and legs were left unprotected. The suit weighed nearly 50 kilos.

The Kelly Gang holding up the police station at the town of Jerilderie.

The masterplan

In June 1880, Kelly devised his criminal masterplan. He intended to lure a trainload of policemen into an **ambush** and topple the train into a deep gully, killing all the police. With all the district's police dead, Kelly planned to rob all the banks in the area.

Ned and his gang planned to wear suits of armour made from plough shares. But his scheme did not go according to plan. The police were warned, escaped the ambush unhurt, and surrounded the hotel where the Kelly Gang was waiting. A fierce gunfight followed.

The final fight

Each member of the Kelly Gang was hit by gunfire. Ned, although wounded, approached the police wearing his armour and firing his guns. Most of the police bullets bounced off the thick armour, but one policeman fired at Ned's unprotected legs and he fell to the ground.

Ned Kelly was charged with murder, found guilty and sentenced to death. He was hanged in Melbourne on 11 November 1880. His last words were, 'Such is life'.

In disguise

On another occasion in the town of Jerilderie, the Kellys locked the police in their cells, put on their uniforms and made one constable introduce them around the town as the new police force. The next day they robbed the bank.

Ned Kelly was eventually captured, tried and sentenced to death. A petition of 60 000 signatures could not save his life.

BILLY THE KID

1859–1881

Billy the Kid started his life of crime when still a child. He became a ruthless gunslinger.

Patrick Henry McCarty also called himself William Bonney and Kid Antrim. But at his death, aged 21, he was known as Billy the Kid, one of the most feared outlaws in the West.

The Kid was born in November in 1859 in New York's East Side. The family moved to Kansas when Billy was a child and his father died there. He then moved with his mother and brother to Colorado where his mother married William H Antrim. The family moved to Silver City, New Mexico. Billy the Kid was an expert card-player by the age of eight and, when he was 12 years old, it is said that he killed a man with a knife for insulting his mother. By the time he was 18 years old, Billy the Kid had been charged with 12 murders.

Cowboy Kid

The Kid became known as an expert who could escape from any jail. The Kid's first escape from jail was when he was 15 years old. He was locked up for stealing laundry, but escaped by climbing up the chimney. He stole a horse and headed for Arizona, hoping to become a cowboy. For the next two years the Kid worked on many sheep and cattle ranches, learning the skills of a professional cowboy.

First victim

The Kid also learned how to use a pistol and a rifle. In 1877, at the age of 17, he became involved in a fight with the local blacksmith. The Kid drew his gun and shot the man, who died the next day. The Kid was charged with murder and put in jail, but he managed to escape and fled to Lincoln County in New Mexico.

A major dispute

The Kid took a job on a ranch owned by an Englishman called John Tunstall. A very strong friendship grew between the Kid and Tunstall that was to be the downfall of the Kid. A major dispute had been growing between Tunstall and another local rancher, who had falsely accused Tunstall of cheating. The authorities took the side of the local rancher against the Englishman.

Cowboys

Two important events in the year for cowboys were the massive cattle round-ups every spring and autumn. Cowboys would **brand** new-born calves and choose cattle to take to the market. Then they began the long drive to a railway for the cattle to be shipped east. On the trail cowboys faced many dangers including wild animals, rustlers (cattle thieves), and stampedes.

The Kid became a cowboy when he left home, working on sheep and cattle ranches.

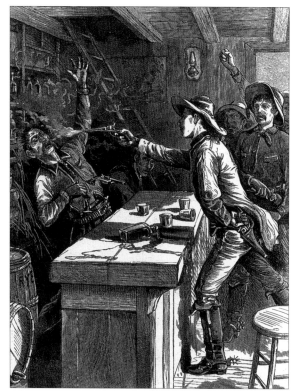

Theft and shootings became a way of life for Billy the Kid when he was on the run from the law.

New Mexico

By now Billy the Kid was on the run and leading a life of cattle stealing and general lawlessness. Pat Garrett, who had been an outlaw and a friend of the Kid's, was elected sheriff with the task of finding Billy the Kid. His posse eventually tracked down the Kid and his gang to a house in New Mexico.

Pat Garrett, a former friend of the Kid's, was given the job of capturing him.

Meaningless death

Tunstall heard that the sheriff and a **posse** were coming after him. Rather than have a gunfight with the local deputy, Tunstall left the ranch with the Kid and his other men. But the deputy and his posse rode after Tunstall, stopped him and shot him dead. The Kid, with the other men from the ranch, looked on helplessly. Billy vowed to avenge Tunstall's death. The next month, the Kid's gang caught up with two of Tunstall's killers on their way to prison with a deputy. The Kid shot them dead and killed the deputy. A few weeks later he shot two more of Tunstall's killers.

Gunfight at the OK Corral

Wyatt Earp (1848-1929) was one of the best-known sheriffs and gunfighters of the American west. He gained his reputation at the famous gunfight at the OK Corral, Tombstone, Arizona, on 26 October, 1881. The three Earp brothers and Wyatt's friend, Doc Holliday, shot dead three members of the Clanton gang in a short but ferocious gunfight. Wyatt Earp was the only one not to be injured.

Starved out of hiding

Garrett's men surrounded the house, making escape impossible. After a few days, when the food and water had run out, Pat Garrett had an idea. He got his men to light a fire and fry food within smelling distance of the house. After a little while the hungry outlaws surrendered. The Kid was imprisoned straight away and in 1881 stood trial accused of three murders.

Final escape

The Kid was found guilty and sentenced to hang. But he managed to escape with the help of a friend who left a gun in an outhouse for him. He shot the two deputies who were guarding him, leaped on a horse and rode off.

That's him!

Pat Garrett was soon back on the Kid's trail. Knowing the places they used to go to as friends, the sheriff guessed rightly that the Kid would head towards the hideout of a friend, Pete Maxwell. Garrett and his posse sneaked up on the place in the middle of the night.

The Kid, who was awake, called to Maxwell because he noticed some strange figures on the porch. A reply came back: 'That's him!' and Garrett shot the Kid just above the heart, killing him instantly.

Billy the Kid was shot just above the heart by his friend turned sheriff, Pat Garrett.

BONNIE AND CLYDE

Clyde Barrow 1909–1934
Bonnie Parker 1910–1934

During the Depression of the 1930s a crimewave swept across America. Among the gangsters responsible for the violence was the young couple Bonnie and Clyde.

Clyde Barrow was born on 24 March 1909. He began to steal when he was 15. He came from a poor background and had a hard childhood. One of his few pleasures was watching cowboy films at the cinema. He imagined himself to be like the outlaw Jesse James.

Bonnie Parker was born on 1 October 1910 in Texas and grew up in Cement City, a tough, run-down area. Bonnie was an intelligent and loving child who adored her mother. But she was also known for her sudden, violent outbursts and her craving for attention.

Love at first sight

Bonnie and Clyde met in January 1930 and were instantly attracted to each other. They soon fell in love. Bonnie was overcome with grief when Clyde was imprisoned for burglary and car theft. She smuggled a gun into jail and with this Clyde managed to escape.

Bonnie Parker and Clyde Barrow first met in January 1930. They soon became two of the most ruthless gangsters in America.

The Great Depression

There were many different reasons for the Great Depression of 1929 to 1934, which had far-reaching effects worldwide. In America nearly 14 million people, about one in four, were unemployed and thousands of businesses went bankrupt. Also, in some areas, the land had been **overfarmed** and had turned to dust. There was no **welfare system** for those who had fallen on hard times. Many turned to crime to make ends meet.

A long prison sentence

A few days later Clyde was arrested again, this time for robbing a railway ticket office at gunpoint. He was sentenced to 14 years imprisonment in a grim Texas prison that was known to be very tough. Not even Bonnie could get him out of this prison, so Clyde came up with his own gruesome plan. He persuaded another prisoner to cut off two of his toes with an axe, hoping the prison authorities would feel sorry for him and let him go. Clyde didn't know that he was already being considered for **parole** and was eventually released.

Life on the road

Once he was out, Clyde rejoined Bonnie. They stole a car, teamed up with three others, and decided to head for West Dallas. The newly-formed gang drove for hundreds of miles, stealing one car after another. They often lived in the car for long periods at a time. Over the next few years, Bonnie and Clyde and their gang robbed many banks, restaurants and filling stations, but their biggest haul was only $3500. During these years they killed 12 people, and become known as one of the most daring and violent gangs of the era.

Unemployed men queue for food in New York during the Depression in the 1930s.

Public Enemy Number One

In 1933, Bonnie and Clyde decided to hide out in Missouri. They were joined by Clyde's brother, Buck, and his wife Blanche. They rented a house and led a quiet life for a couple of weeks until the neighbours became suspicious and informed the police.

The house was surrounded and a shoot-out followed, which left two police officers dead and Clyde slightly injured. The gang escaped and the authorities put every available person on the job of capturing Bonnie and Clyde, dead or alive. Clyde was given the title Public Enemy Number One of the southwest. They were chased around the country as they continued to commit crime after crime.

A bloody attack

In February 1934 the chase ended when the gang was again surrounded by the police, this time in Missouri. Bonnie and Clyde managed to escape following a fierce gunfight, but this time the police caused serious casualties. Buck was riddled with bullets and died in hospital six days later. Blanche, who was shot and blinded, decided to stay with her husband. She was eventually charged and sent to trial and was sentenced to ten years in prison.

Bonnie and Clyde photographed each other while on the run from the law.

Clyde was declared Public Enemy Number One of the southwest in 1933.

Pretty Boy Floyd

Pretty Boy Floyd (1901–1934), was a tall, handsome labourer from Oklahoma who turned to crime during the Great Depression. Floyd robbed banks and shot anybody who got in his way. It is said that he killed ten people. He was gunned down by the **FBI** in Ohio. Like Bonnie and Clyde, Floyd became a **legend**. Once, when he was on the run, he was fed by a poor farming family. When he left, the farmer's wife found a thousand dollar note under his empty plate.

Fatal ambush

Bonnie and Clyde stayed on the run for the next three months. A lawman called Frank Hamer trailed them across nine states. On 23 May 1934, acting on information from a former gang member, Hamer and five other lawmen set up an **ambush** outside Arcadia, Louisiana.

Riddled with bullets

Bonnie and Clyde were killed as the Ford V8 they were driving was riddled with holes from nearly one hundred rounds of **ammunition**. Their bodies were put on display in a local furniture shop. Thousands of people went to see the corpses of the most famous gangster couple in history.

The bullet-riddled Ford Sedan car in which Bonnie and Clyde died is on show in Las Vegas.

GLOSSARY

Alias A made-up name used by criminals and other outlaws when they want to keep their identity a secret.

Allegiance A person's loyalty to a king or queen or a country.

American Civil War A civil war is a war between people of the same country. The American Civil War was fought between the northern and southern states of America. The southern states wanted to keep slavery and thought they should have more power to govern themselves. The northern states wanted to ban slavery and felt the president should rule the whole country equally.

Ambush A surprise attack from a concealed place.

Ammunition Bullets and cannon balls which are fired from guns and cannons.

Assassin Someone who murders a famous person.

Blockade To cut off a place by surrounding it with ships or troops.

Bootlegging Making and selling something illegally.

Bow The front part of a ship.

Brand The owner's mark on cattle.

Canton A political division of Switzerland.

Confederation A collection of states united into one area or country.

Cutlass A broad, curved sword with a short handle.

Exile To force a person to leave his or her home or country.

FBI Federal Bureau of Investigation, part of the Justice Department in the USA.

Footboy A boy servant.

Foot regiment A group of soldiers that travels on foot rather than by ship or horse.

Fortress A large castle well protected from enemies.

Frigate A medium-sized war ship.

Governor A person sent to organize and rule a country in place of the king or queen.

Guerrilla A fighter who wages war by ambush and surprise attack.

HMS His or Her Majesty's Ship.

Homestead A small house and plot of land.

Immigrants People who have left their own country to go and live in another country.

Jacobites The supporters of James II of England after his removal from the throne in 1688.

King's Flag The flag of a ruling king or queen under which a ship sails.

Legend A very old story passed down from generation to generation that may or may not be true.

Medieval The period of history between 1100 AD and 1500 AD. It is also called the Middle Ages.

Native Americans The original inhabitants of America before Europeans arrived.

Overfarmed Land which has been exhausted by growing crops.

Pardon To forgive or excuse a person for a crime by not punishing them.

Parole When a prisoner is released from jail before his prison sentence is finished, usually for good behaviour.

Peasant A farm worker who usually earns little money.

Plunder To steal valuable goods by force.

Posse A group of people who ride out with the sheriff or another lawman to search for outlaws.

Priory The name of a building where nuns or monks live.

Privateer A sailor on a privately-owned ship used by a government to attack enemy ships in time of war.

Red Cross The international organization which provides medical care for victims of war and natural disasters.

Resistance A group of people who fight against an enemy force in their country.

Rustling To steal horses and cattle.

Seal A ring decorated with the badge or emblem of the king.

Spanish Succession The war fought between 1701-13 by the major European countries for control of Spain and its empire.

Tenant A peasant farmer who leased farmland from a landowner. In return the tenant would work for the landlord and fight for him in times of war.

Traitor A person who betrays their country.

Welfare system A system set up by the government to help people who have fallen on hard times.

INDEX